Higher ENGLISH for CfE

CRITICAL READING

Carolyn Cunningham

D0547784

SCOTTISH
EXAMINATION
MATERIALS

HODDER
GIBSON
AN HACHETTE UK COMPANY

Thanks to Davie

The Publishers would like to thank the following for permission to reproduce copyright material:

Photo credits p.iv © Rido – Fotolia; **p.x** © Dirima – Fotolia; **p.1** © By permission of the Estate of Ena Lamont Stewart; **p.11** (top) © Geraint Lewis/Alamy, (bottom) © Geraint Lewis/Alamy; **p.19** © NCAimages – Fotolia; **p.21** © Lewis Grassic Gibbon Centre; **p.31** © Anglia Images/Alamy; **p.32** © Rafa Irusta Machin / Fotolia; **p.40** © Algol – Fotolia; **p.43** (top) © Werner Forman Archive/Heritage Image Partnership Ltd /Alamy, (bottom) © westrayart – Fotolia; **p.57** © starush – Fotolia; **p.65** © Georgios Kollidas – Fotolia; **p.68** © Ornitolog82 – Fotolia; **p.76** © millaf – Fotolia; **p.87** © Geraint Lewis/Alamy; **p.90** © Philip Gendreau/Bettman/Corbis; **p.92** © Fergus Mackay/Alamy; **p.102** © LoloStock – Fotolia; **p.103** © Monkey Business – Fotolia.

Chapter opener image reproduced on pages iv, 1, 21, 43, 65, 87 and 112 © Tyler Olson – Fotolia.com.

Acknowledgements Extracts from 'Some Old Photographs' and 'The Bargain' from *A Choosing: Selected Poems* by Liz Lochhead are reproduced by permission of Polygon, an imprint of Birlinn Ltd (www.birlinn.co.uk).

Every effort has been made to trace all copyright holders, but if any have been inadvertently overlooked the Publishers will be pleased to make the necessary arrangements at the first opportunity.

Although every effort has been made to ensure that website addresses are correct at time of going to press, Hodder Gibson cannot be held responsible for the content of any website mentioned in this book. It is sometimes possible to find a relocated web page by typing in the address of the home page for a website in the URL window of your browser.

Orders: please contact Bookpoint Ltd, 130 Park Drive, Abingdon, Oxon OX14 4SE. Telephone: (44) 01235 827720. Fax: (44) 01235 400454. Lines are open 9.00–5.00, Monday to Saturday, with a 24-hour message answering service. Visit our website at www.hoddereducation.co.uk. Hodder Gibson can be contacted direct on: Tel: 0141 848 1609; Fax: 0141 889 6315; email: hoddergibson@hodder.co.uk

© Carolyn Cunningham 2015

First published in 2015 by
Hodder Gibson, an imprint of Hodder Education,
An Hachette UK Company
2a Christie Street
Paisley PA1 1NB

Impression number	5	4	3	2	1	
Year		2019	2018	2017	2016	2015

All rights reserved. Apart from any use permitted under UK copyright law, no part of this publication may be reproduced or transmitted in any form or by any means, electronic or mechanical, including photocopying and recording, or held within any information storage and retrieval system, without permission in writing from the publisher or under licence from the Copyright Licensing Agency Limited. Further details of such licences (for reprographic reproduction) may be obtained from the Copyright Licensing Agency Limited, Saffron House, 6–10 Kirby Street, London EC1N 8TS.

Cover photo © Tyler Olson – Fotolia.com
Illustrations by Barking Dog Art Design and Illustration
Typeset in 12/14.5pt Minion Regular by Integra Software Services Pvt. Ltd., Pondicherry, India
Printed in Spain

A catalogue record for this title is available from the British Library

ISBN: 978 1 4718 3800 2

CONTENTS

INTRODUCTION

Your Higher English exam is made up of:

* Portfolio: Writing (30%)

* Exam Paper 1: Reading for Understanding, Analysis and Evaluation (30%)

* Exam Paper 2: Critical Reading (40%).

This means that the Critical Reading component is the single most important part of the Higher course. This book contains everything you need to succeed in the Critical Reading exam (except the actual texts!). It includes:

* notes on key drama, prose and poetry texts to increase your knowledge

* activities to develop your analysis skills

* worked examples of types of questions

* advice on how to approach analysis and essay writing

* sample plans and essays

* exam tips.

In using this book you will build your confidence, which will enable you to perform well on the day and gain those extra marks, to help you achieve the grade you need.

What is critical reading?

Critical reading is the study of literature, non-fiction writing, media and language. It makes use of your skills in understanding, analysis and evaluation. If you are studying a play, novel, poem or media text, you are developing your analysis skills. The 'critical' part does not mean 'criticism' in the normal sense of pointing out the 'bad' aspects of something; instead, it means using your critical faculty – your ability to analyse and comment on features such as plot, characters, theme and techniques used by the writer.

Whenever you read, discuss or do class activities on literature, make your own notes, find quotations to link aspects of character or theme, do presentations or quizzes with classmates – you are developing your critical reading skills. This book will help you both in class or studying at home, with friends or on your own.

Why study Scottish literature?

The study of Scottish literature is now compulsory in Scottish schools, as part of the new National 5 and Higher English qualifications. The idea behind including a Scottish writer or text as compulsory in the new courses is to encourage all young people in Scotland to learn about, appreciate and enjoy the literature which is part of our culture.

To make it manageable and to allow questions on specific texts, Scottish Qualifications Authority (SQA) drew up a list of writers and texts in the three genres of drama, prose (novels and short stories) and poetry. The list is wide and combines both traditional and modern texts, both male and female writers, and authors from different geographical locations within Scotland. Your teacher will have chosen texts that are appropriate for you and your class. These will probably be ones that he or she really likes and, perhaps, ones about which he or she has expert knowledge.

There are many brilliant writers in Scotland and the list contains fourteen. Of course, there are many magnificent writers and texts that were not included in the list this time. The plan is to revise the list in the coming years, to give other writers a turn. Maybe someone reading this textbook will be on the list in the future!

The texts

As part of your Higher course, you will be studying something from the following list: at least one (and possibly two or even three) from the list. Some of the texts are long – novels and plays – and some are shorter – short stories or poems. If you are studying the poetry or short stories of a writer, you will be studying six texts by him or her.

Drama

- **The Cheviot, the Stag and the Black, Black Oil** by John McGrath
- **Men Should Weep** by Ena Lamont Stewart
- **The Slab Boys** by John Byrne

Prose

- **Six short stories** by Iain Crichton Smith ('The Red Door', 'The Telegram', 'Mother and Son', 'In Church', 'The Painter', 'The Crater')
- **Six short stories** by George Mackay Brown ('A Time to Keep', 'The Whaler's Return', 'The Wireless Set', 'The Bright Spade', 'Tartan', 'The Eye of the Hurricane')
- **The Cone-Gatherers** by Robin Jenkins
- **Sunset Song** by Lewis Grassic Gibbon
- **The Trick is to Keep Breathing** by Janice Galloway

Poetry

- **Robert Burns** ('To a Mouse', 'Holy Willie's Prayer', 'A Poet's Welcome to his Love-Begotten Daughter', 'Address to the Deil', 'Tam o' Shanter', 'A Man's a Man for A' That')
- **Carol Ann Duffy** ('War Photographer', 'Havisham', 'Valentine', 'Originally', 'Anne Hathaway', 'Mrs Midas')
- **Liz Lochhead** ('Some Old Photographs', 'The Bargain', 'View of Scotland/Love Poem', 'For my Grandmother Knitting', 'My Rival's House', 'Last Supper')

- **Norman MacCaig** ('Sounds of the Day', 'Assisi', 'Visiting Hour', 'Memorial', 'Aunt Julia', 'Basking Shark')
- **Sorley MacLean** ('Hallaig', 'Screapadal', 'Heroes', 'Shores', 'An Autumn Day', 'I Gave You Immortality')
- **Don Paterson** ('Waking with Russell', 'The Thread', '11:00: Baldovan', 'Two Trees', 'The Ferryman's Arms', 'Nil Nil')

If you have studied National 5, you may already have encountered *The Cone-Gatherers*, Iain Crichton Smith, Carol Ann Duffy or Norman MacCaig. This is because these texts/writers are 'crossover' texts/writers: they appear at both National 5 and Higher levels.

The Critical Reading exam

The Critical Reading exam lasts for 1 hour 30 minutes. It has two sections and you should spend about 45 minutes on each section. If you have already studied National 5 English, this format will be familiar to you. The two sections of the exam are the Scottish Text and the Critical Essay. Each is worth 20% of the total marks for the Higher qualification.

If you have studied only one text from the SQA Scottish text list, you must use that text for the Scottish Text questions. You may choose from other literature you have studied for the Critical Essay section. You must *not* answer on the same text or the same genre for both sections.

If you have studied more than one text from the Scottish text list, you will choose one of these for the Scottish Text questions and may use your other Scottish text (or other literature you have studied) for the Critical Essay section. You must *not* answer on the same text or the same genre for both sections of the paper.

Higher students often study something from each of the three major genres: prose, drama and poetry. This depends on which texts you study though (some are very long) and other factors like how many times a week you have English in school, so do not panic if you are studying only two genres. Your teacher will have worked out what is best for you and your class.

For example, if you have studied:

- Drama: *Romeo and Juliet* (other literature)
- Prose: *Sunset Song* (SQA list)
- Poetry: by Philip Larkin (other literature)

then you must answer on *Sunset Song* in the Scottish Text section and then can choose either *Romeo and Juliet* or Philip Larkin's poetry for the Critical Essay question.

On the other hand, if you have studied:

- Drama: *Men Should Weep* (SQA list)
- Prose: *The Picture of Dorian Gray* (other literature)
- Poetry: by Robert Burns (SQA list)

you can choose between Burns and *Men Should Weep* for the Scottish Text section and then choose between *The Picture of Dorian Gray* and whichever Scottish one you did not choose before for your critical essay.

You may even have studied all three genres from the list, such as:

- Drama: *Men Should Weep*
- Prose: George Mackay Brown's short stories
- Poetry: by Liz Lochhead.

Some approaches to exam questions apply to all genres you may study. However, many of the challenges you will face will be genre-specific. How you tackle the Scottish text question will vary too, depending on whether you are studying one long text (for example, a novel) or a selection of shorter texts (for example, short stories).

How are the Scottish text questions marked?

- They are marked out of a total of 20 marks, with 10 marks awarded for questions on the text or extract used in the exam and 10 marks which 'go beyond', enabling you to show your wider knowledge of the text (if it is a novel or play) or of the other texts you have studied by the same writer (if it is a poem or short story).

- There are approximately five questions. The final question is worth 10 marks. The others are usually worth 2, 3 or 4 marks.

- The shorter questions will test your understanding of the text/extract and your ability to analyse techniques used in it.

- The general 'rule' of marking the shorter questions is: 2 marks for a detailed/insightful comment plus a quotation/reference; 1 mark for more basic comment plus a quotation/reference; 0 marks for a quotation/reference with no comment.

- The 10-mark question is broken up by markers into 2, 2 and 6 marks:
  - 2 marks are available for explaining the link mentioned in the question between this text or extract and other texts/parts of longer text. The SQA calls this 'commonality' (i.e. what they have in common)
  - 2 marks are for linking this to the text or extract in the exam
  - 6 marks are for linking this to other texts or parts of a longer text. These 6 marks for wider knowledge can be gained, for example, by three well-developed, detailed/insightful points plus a quotation/reference – for 2 marks each.

How to use this book

This book covers both sections of the Critical Reading exam:

1. Scottish Text Question: there are chapters on five of the Scottish texts on the list, but, whichever texts you have studied, the approaches in this book will be helpful to you. With your teacher you will have studied at least one of the fourteen texts/writers on the SQA list. You can be confident that your particular writer or text will come up in the exam.

2. Critical Essay: this section includes advice, tips and sample essays/plans on a selection of genres. Whatever you have studied, this will be helpful in preparing you for the exam. In the exam you will choose one essay from a list (divided into genre groups). These essay questions will fit a broad range of texts: they do not name specific texts but allow you to choose something you have studied and apply the question to that text. The essay can be written on a text from the Scottish text list, but only if you have studied more than one text on the list. Remember, you will definitely need one of the texts on the list for your Scottish text question.

This book includes a selection of different genres, and longer and shorter texts, as well as a mixture of traditional and modern examples. It focuses on:

- Drama: **Men Should Weep** by Ena Lamont Stewart
- Prose (novel): **Sunset Song** by Lewis Grassic Gibbon
- Prose (short stories): **George Mackay Brown** selection
- Poetry: **Robert Burns** selection and **Liz Lochhead** selection.

As you progress through the book, the tasks and questions are designed to help you:

- reinforce your confident knowledge of the texts
- develop your analysis skills
- make connections within the longer texts (for example, characters, theme, plot and setting) and between the shorter texts. This is important for the final 10-mark question in the exam.

The questions can be done on your own, with a partner or in small groups. Some focus on one specific area of analysis and some are broader. Marking schemes are also included.

Genres

Drama

There are three plays on the Scottish text list. If you are studying a play, whichever one it is, you will focus on:

- narrative
- characters
- setting
- theme
- dramatic techniques such as structure.

The interplay of these features gives meaning to the text. For example, in *Men Should Weep*, the setting is vital to our understanding of theme and characters.

Remember that a play is written to be performed and there will be aspects specific to the genre – features you would see only in a play (such as stage directions) – just because it is a play.

Prose: novels

There are three novels on the Scottish text list. If you are studying a novel, whichever one it is, you will focus on the following important elements:

- narrative structure
- characters
- setting
- theme
- style.

As with drama, the interplay between the different elements creates meaning. For example, in *Sunset Song*, the setting helps create meaning in terms of theme and characters.

Strictly speaking, these kinds of divisions are artificial: after all, we experience a play or a novel as a whole when watching or reading it. However, dividing it into aspects such as these does make it manageable – which, of course, helps you to study it for your exam.

Prose: short stories

There are two collections of short stories on the list. If you are studying one of these, you will focus on each individual story (narrative, character, setting, theme and style/structure) and also, vitally, the links between them. You might think that short stories would be simpler than a longer novel, but length can be deceptive. The stories on the list are just as complex as the novels but distilled into a short, intense burst of writing.

Poetry

Poetry is particularly well represented on the list. Depending on the poem, you will be focusing on some of these elements:

* characters
* narrative
* theme
* persona – the 'speaking voice' of the poem
* structure and verse form
* imagery
* sound effects
* contrast
* other poetic techniques.

As you can see, a major focus in the study of poetry is the analysis of techniques. You may be studying a traditional poet like Robert Burns or someone more modern like Liz Lochhead, but do not think that a poem is easy just because it is written in more modern language. All the poems chosen for the Higher course are complex and all require detailed and perceptive study.

Remember that to do your best in the exam you will need to:

* have a confident knowledge of the texts
* develop your analysis skills
* practise analysis questions and critical essays.

This book will help you do all three.

Top tips for success

Remember to prepare for your Critical Reading exam!

- Know your texts confidently and thoroughly.
- Practise your analysis skills and critical essay writing.
- Prepare well so that you know what to expect from your exam, both for the Scottish Text and for the Critical Essay sections.
- You cannot 'second guess' which extract or shorter text will be chosen for the exam. Develop your rich knowledge and analytical skills so that you can deal with any extract or text.
- Keep making connections between the shorter texts and within the longer ones.
- Make revision notes on your literary texts (for example, character, theme, setting, techniques), then summarise them. Try to cut them down to five key points on, for example, a character or theme. Remember these, and then build on them in the exam.
- Give yourself plenty of time to study and to practise key areas like essay planning and writing.
- Do not panic! Your Scottish text will definitely come up in the exam. The Critical Essay questions will offer you a range of good options for your text.

This book will help you succeed in the Critical Reading exam. Good luck – and keep reading Scottish literature!

DRAMA: *MEN SHOULD WEEP*

BY ENA LAMONT STEWART

Task

On your own

To prepare for your work on this play, carry out some background research on the internet by searching for 'the Depression (1930s)'.

If you have the chance to see a performance of this moving, funny and deeply thought-provoking play, seize it. Written by Ena Lamont Stewart in 1947 and successfully revived by the 7:84 Theatre Company in 1982, it is set in 1930s Glasgow (the time of the Great Depression) and deals with major themes that are all too relevant today: poverty, suffering and injustice. It also deals with heroism of the human spirit, shown through Maggie, the main character. She is at the heart of the play – just as she is at the heart of the Morrison family.

We will start with an overview of some of the play's main features and concerns. You may have read the whole play before starting on this chapter, or you may be reading the play in class and working through this book at the same time: the activities are designed to be flexible. The next few pages deal with the whole play, so watch out for 'spoilers' if you have not read it yet. They can be useful revision exercises later.

Plot

The action of the play takes place over the few weeks leading up to Christmas. At this time, we follow the fortunes and misfortunes of the Morrison family. These include struggling with unemployment, relationship issues and illness. The various plot strands build up to a climax as Maggie comes under increasing pressure to hold the family together. There are three acts:

- Act 1 sets the scene and establishes the major themes of the play.

- Act 2 develops these as tensions and problems within the family worsen.

- Act 3 sees the climax as Maggie finally 'snaps' and asserts herself, and the resolution as the Morrisons face a future which is hopeful in a muted way. There's certainly not a 'happy-ever-after' ending.

There are five scenes in the play: we will look at each individually and also draw the scenes together.

With a partner or in small groups

Take one act of the play each (or divide up scenes, depending on numbers working together) and note down three key events that happen in each act. Then get back together and compile your skeleton plan of the play. Be prepared to justify your choices to the rest of the group. There are more than three key events in each act, so there are plenty of possible correct answers.

Possible answers

Act 1

- Lily arrives, providing beans, advice and criticism.
- John and Lily argue. She leaves.
- Isa and Alec move in.
- Jenny arrives home late. Argument with John.

Act 2

- Lizzie arrives to collect Granny – and to complain.
- Maggie comes back from hospital very upset.
- Jenny leaves home.
- Alec and Isa come in after committing a robbery – they argue. Alec becomes violent.
- Maggie sides with Alec – and hits Isa.
- Isa flirts with John.
- Maggie loses control.

Act 3

- John gives Maggie new hat.
- Lily takes Maggie shopping.
- Confrontation between Alec and Isa. Alec attacks Isa. Isa leaves Alec.
- Jenny returns with offer of money for a house.
- Maggie asserts herself and accepts although John disagrees.

Setting

The whole play takes place in the main room of the Morrisons' tenement flat in the East End of Glasgow in the 1930s. This consists of a combined living room, kitchen and bedroom (for Maggie and John), leading off to the other bedroom, the 'back parlour' and a bed recess. This limited space is home to (as well as Maggie and John) their children Jenny, Edie, Ernest, Bertie, Marina and Christopher, as well as Granny and, later, Alec and Isa. That's eleven people living in three rooms and a recess! And within those eleven residents, we have an elderly person, a baby and a seriously ill child. It is easy to see why tempers flare and tension rises: no privacy, no comfort – not even a bed to call their own – except for Granny, who takes her bed as she travels between Maggie and the less welcoming Lizzie (and her bed is all she can call her own!). The claustrophobic nature of the setting is of course integral to the development of plot, theme and character. This play would not have worked in a more spacious, luxurious setting. The narrow limits of the flat can be seen to symbolise the limited options and opportunities of the characters: Jenny, for example, cannot live the life she wants in the close and – with its damp and dirt – it is literally killing Bertie.

Characters

The other characters all relate to Maggie in some way, as shown in the diagram below.

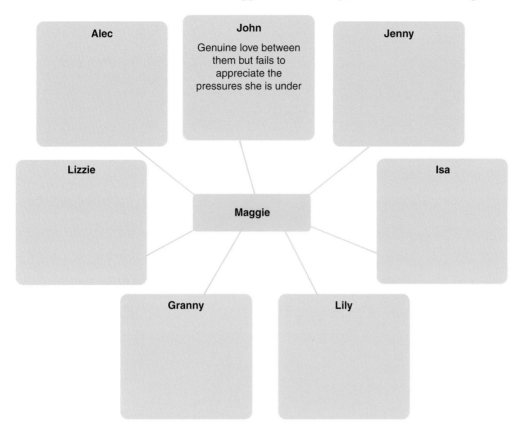

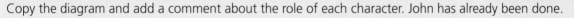

Task

With a partner

Copy the diagram and add a comment about the role of each character. John has already been done.

Characters as individuals, the interplay between them and how they relate to themes of the play form a significant part of this study.

Themes

What relevance does a play written in 1947 and set in 1930 have today? Simply, the major themes of the play are universal. People are still poor in the UK and throughout the world; people want the best for those they love, but do not always show it well – and ordinary people are still heroic. The major themes of the play are:

- poverty
- the roles of men and women
- human heroism.

1. Poverty

Poverty is demonstrated in the play through the following features:

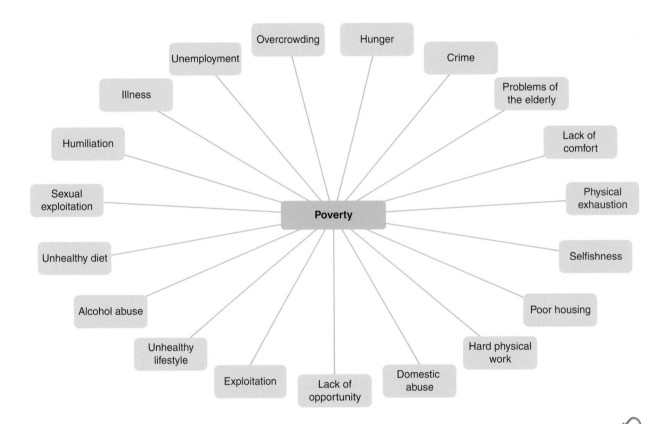

Task

On your own

Choose five of the elements of poverty given in the diagram. Find examples of these in the text (including quotations), and note down how your examples illustrate the theme of poverty. Can you add any positive aspects of Maggie's life, her family and her neighbours?

Discussion

There are many examples of the negatives of poverty throughout the play. One positive aspect of their way of life is the way the neighbours support one another – both in a crisis and in day-to-day matters. They genuinely understand what each other is going through, although that does not mean they don't fall out a lot too!

2. The roles of men and women

The 1930s in the East End of Glasgow was a time of traditional roles: people did not have the freedom to question assumptions based on gender that we enjoy today. The table opposite gives some of the assumptions that were accepted in those days.

Men	Women
Head of the household – should be figure of authority	Lives are linked to the home, husband and children
Should provide for the family	Limited choices and aspirations
Should be the 'boss' in relationships with women	Wives must accept what husbands decide, including physical violence
No housework – demeaning	Undertake all housework, even if working outside the home too
No caring duties	Undertake caring duties for children and the elderly
Sexual desire to be expected	Sexual lives dominated or exploited by men
'Allowed' to express principles openly	Dressing flamboyantly is criticised (even Maggie's red hat causes comments)
Critical of women	Critical of men
Should not show tender emotions, although anger was OK!	Comradeship of other women, but no privacy
Alcohol and gambling to be expected	Drinking alcohol is criticised

Thankfully, most of these assumptions have now changed. To understand the Morrisons fully, we have to be aware of how different their attitudes are to ours today. For example, it seems obvious now that, as John is unemployed and Maggie has a cleaning job outside the home, John should take on the main chores of the home. But no – to him that would have been humiliating, emphasising even more his 'failure' as a man. So Maggie does it all.

With a partner

1. Looking at the table above, show how both Maggie and John can be said to be trapped in or frustrated by the gender roles expected of them. Choose one other character and show how he or she is trapped.
2. Maggie lives in a world that is, largely, female. (Comparing the numbers of male and female characters in the play demonstrates this.) Compare the key female characters of Maggie, Lily, Lizzie, Granny, Jenny and Isa. What sort of different stresses and difficulties do they experience? How do they cope?
3. What are your initial impressions of the male characters? Do you feel the play presents a stereotypical view of men?

Discussion

1. Although Maggie is the one more obviously trapped in the role of home-maker and carer, with very little money or support to help her, and struggles throughout the play to do right by her family (and there are many examples), John could also be said to be trapped. The 1930s was a time of major unemployment, when unskilled workers like John found getting work very hard. We can see the frustration and shame he feels.
2. The female characters have the double problem of poverty and gender. Women are expected to put up with and support their men: they have even less power over their lives than poor men. Granny has the extra problem of age: she has outlived her usefulness and is now living out her days as a burden on her family (she is welcome up to a point with Maggie and John, but less so with Lizzie). Lily and Lizzie are noticeably more powerful: Lily unmarried; Lizzie a widow. Both have more disposable income, although Lizzie has turned to exploitation and crime to make herself comfortable. Isa rebels against her role of wife to a man she despises, but her solution is to swap

him for another man. Even Jenny, young and determined, finds happiness through a relationship with a man that, because of the lack of legal recognition through marriage, is hopeful but insecure.

3. The only male characters (apart from the removal men who criticise Isa for her cheek to Granny) are John, Alec and Ernest. They can be seen as 'types' up to a point. John is an idealist who, until Act 3, does not manage to deal with practical problems and is not above flirting with his own daughter-in-law. Alec is an unappreciative 'mummy's boy' who manipulates his mother into giving him money and sympathy. He is also a pathetically devoted husband who will do anything – even commit crime – for the scornful Isa. Even Ernest can be seen to be developing into a male 'type': while his sister comes in to help with food and Granny, he carries on playing, as he does not need to follow the domestic rules.

3. Human heroism

As well as being a realistic character, Maggie is a symbol of heroism, of woman and of humanity. How does this work?

Task

With a partner

The table below gives a detailed breakdown of Maggie's heroism. Find an example for each of the following aspects. There are many examples and there may be some overlap.

Aspect	Example
Keeps going, despite repeated disappointments	She discovers that Alec has taken most of her money, but continues to get food for the family and tries to hide her feelings
Makes unfortunate people welcome	
Deals with physical exhaustion	
Denies herself food	
Cares for those who are physically dependent	
Practical rather than idealistic – does not have the luxury of ideals	
Loyal, even when she has been let down	
Optimistic about the future	
Tries to set standards	
Forces herself to do things that upset her	
Shows humour in adversity	
Shows appreciation of help	
Holds on to her belief in people	
Remembers happy past times positively, rather than despairing about the future	
Does not expect thanks or appreciation	
Tries to be cheerful	
Tries to keep the peace	

Of course, Maggie is not perfect. She is a realistic, unsentimental portrayal of a human being. She does not manage to be heroic all the time: she gets angry, tired, exasperated and critical – but we are 'on her side'. One of the ways Lamont Stewart achieves this is by offering us other characters to compare her with. We will look at these later.

Task

On your own
Can you think of examples of Maggie's less heroic behaviour? Aim for three.

Discussion
1. Maggie is easily manipulated by Alec, whose transparent exploitation of her – even stealing money from her purse – she tries not to see. At one point in Act 2 she is forced to face this heartbreaking truth.
2. She is relentlessly critical of Isa (who 'stole' her boy). Although this is understandable – Isa certainly does plenty to deserve criticism – Maggie sees nothing but faults in Isa (and nothing but good in Alec).
3. She delays taking Bertie to the hospital for his treatment because she cannot cope with it. She refuses to see the truth: that he is dangerously ill with tuberculosis and that he will die if something is not done about their appalling housing.
4. Although she looks after Granny as best she can, she is at times irritable and impatient with her. This is perhaps understandable: Granny, though pitiful and powerless, spends a lot of time complaining.

The themes intertwined
You will have noticed that the three key themes of poverty, gender roles and heroism are intertwined. For example, the challenges Maggie faces are due, to a large extent, to her poverty and gender.

Final general points on the play:

- Remember that this is a play, written to be watched. This means that stage directions and set description will also be important in analysis and could be the focus of questions in your Scottish Text section.

- Most of what has been said so far makes this play seem pretty grim. It is tragic and painful in many parts, but remember it is also funny. Humour is often used as a coping mechanism in difficult situations, and we see Maggie and others making the best of a difficult life through humour.

- It is, of course, a vital part of this play's effect and meaning that it is written in Scots. This might mean an added challenge for you when reading. The particular form of Scots language used is specific to both time and place: Glasgow in the 1930s. Even if you are from the west of Scotland yourself, you may encounter words and expressions unfamiliar to you, as language changes over time. This use of language is, like the setting, integral to the development of theme and character and a vital part of the creation of a realistic world.

Act 1, Scene 1

We will see how the general comments about the play above actually work in the text by examining the opening of the play. If you have not already done so, read Act 1, Scene 1 (including the text in italics at the start) up to the arrival of Lily ('… a brisk knock on the outside door').

Task

In small groups

The opening is significant in terms of:

- setting
- stage directions
- plot
- character development
- thematic development.

Each person in the group should take one or two features of the opening of Act 1 and note down his or her impressions. Then get together to share your ideas. What do we learn from the play's opening?

Possible answers

- **Setting:** overcrowding, with no privacy and little comfort, established immediately with the description of the kitchen, with the bed recess, nappies drying over the fire, clutter and the presence of three generations living so closely together.
- **Stage directions:** we first see Maggie hanging out of the window, shouting at the children outside, while also dealing with Granny's needs and then those of the children, behind the curtain. These attempts to assert some sort of control over the people she is responsible for are the pattern for Maggie's struggle throughout the play. The plight of Granny, infirm and homeless (if it were not for the care of the family who struggle to look after her), is shown in her sitting 'whining and rocking', 'setting up a terrible wail', while her sudden and random singing emphasises her confusion. Edie, though only eleven, is already taking on many family responsibilities. She is dressed in cast-off clothes, messy and skinny. We can see their impoverished diet: sugar and carbohydrate-based, even for the baby. Maggie herself moves between various family needs, except when she 'sinks into a chair and sighs, then yawns widely': her exhaustion is clear.
- **Plot:** Maggie is trying simultaneously to get Granny to bed and her younger children in, fed and ready for bed. We learn that Granny has no home of her own but goes between Maggie and Lizzie, both daughters-in-law, and that Lizzie is reluctant to take her. Maggie clearly is struggling to deal with the various family needs and is in a muddle. She has no time for herself. A 'brisk knock' announces the arrival of Lily.
- **Character development:** Maggie's weary struggles are at the centre of this opening (as, indeed, of the whole play). Her impotent shouting at the children, her conversation with Granny (in which there is limited 'real' communication) and her threats to Edie and Marina suggest an irritable person, but it is the difficulties of her life that make her so. We sense she is 'never finished' and never quite accomplishes anything. She is exasperated and impatient with Granny and her humour can be cutting: 'Och, it's [Granny's life] been ebbin ever since I met ye; but the tide aye seems tae come in again.' Nonetheless, she shows kindness, agreeing to bring Granny tea, with condensed milk, sugar and bread (although this is also a bribe to get her off to bed), and saying, 'John and me wad never send ye onywhere.' Granny is pathetic, needy and manipulative. This suggests that the future for women such as her, when her children have grown up, is bleak and insecure.
- **Thematic development:** all of the above emphasises the difficulties of a life of poverty. We can see that the various characters are actually hungry in a way most of us today do not experience. In the domestic setting this poverty impacts particularly on women, whose life is portrayed as an endless struggle. (Only female characters have appeared so far.) As Maggie says, 'If a woman did everything that ought tae be done aboot the hoose, she'd go on a day an a night till she drapped doon deid.'

Now read the rest of Act 1, Scene 1 if you have not already done so. This falls into three overlapping sections:

- Maggie and Lily
- Maggie, Lily and John
- the neighbours.

Maggie and Lily

In small groups

Maggie's and Lily's lives, attitudes and personalities contrast sharply. Your task is to find quotations that illustrate this contrast using the table below to help focus your search.

Maggie	Quotation	Lily	Quotation
Seems helpless and caught up in muddle		Is exasperated by Maggie's inability to sort things out	
Will not accept that Lily knows better		Wants to provide practical help but feels Maggie is a bit hopeless	
Supports John's explanation for their poverty – it is not their fault		Dismisses John's explanation of their poverty as an excuse	
Refuses to accept that they are to blame for their large family		Blames John for his large family	
Defends her own methods		Criticises Maggie's way of doing things	
Stands up for herself and is not afraid to be cheeky		Criticises the way Maggie looks	
Defends John		Is suspicious of John	

Possible answers

Maggie	Quotation	Lily	Quotation
Seems helpless and caught up in muddle	*'Goad, if it's nae yin, it's anither'*	Is exasperated by Maggie's inability to sort things out	*'Maggie, ye're aye in the same pickle'*
Will not accept that Lily knows better	*'Old maids are awfu good at the criticizin'*	Wants to provide practical help but feels Maggie is a bit hopeless	*'Surveys Maggie's muddle, sighs ... wonders where to start'*
Supports John's explanation for their poverty – it is not their fault	*'I dinna ken whit they dirty rotten buggers in Parliament are doing wi ma money ... John says'*	Dismisses John's explanation of their poverty as an excuse	*'I'm no wantin to hear whit John says aboot they bliddy capitalists'*
Refuses to accept that they are to blame for their large family	*'He's a man and I'm a wumman. We're flesh and blood'*	Blames John for his large family	*'John should think shame o himsel'*
Defends her own methods	*'Awa for Goad's sake! It's no Setterday nicht'*	Criticises Maggie's way of doing things	*'D'ye no tak aff her dress tae wash her neck?'*
Stands up for herself and is not afraid to be cheeky	*'I canna help ma looks ony mair than you can help yours'*	Criticises the way Maggie looks	*'Heve ye looked in the mirror since ye rose the morn?'*
Defends John	*'You leave John alane! He does his best for us'*	Is suspicious of John	*'That's whit he tells you, onyway'*

Maggie, Lily and John

With a partner

Look for positives and negatives in the presentation of John. Try to find three of each. Look particularly at his relationship with Maggie, his attitude to gender roles (remember that no one in the 1930s would have called it that) and his behaviour towards Lily.

Possible answers

Positives	Negatives
Affectionate to Maggie	Dismissive of women: 'nae system'
Welcoming (slightly sarcastic)	Will not go to hospital with Maggie
Sense of humour	Not very appreciative of Lily's help
Helps Maggie – sometimes	Antagonises Lily
Would like to provide Maggie with more	Loses temper
Warm memories of the past	Unfairly critical of Maggie

The neighbours

On your own

In a paragraph or a series of bullet points, write a summary of ways in which the neighbours act as a positive and/or negative force in the lives of women like Maggie.

Discussion

The neighbours provide support, chat, conviviality and understanding towards each other. This would be an important feature in a hard and difficult life. With such polarised gender roles, these women's lives would have little in common with those of their own husbands – and far more of a link with other women. However, they also squabble among themselves: for example, Maggie passes on the teacher's comment about 'beasts' to Mrs Harris, while Mrs Harris accuses Maggie of not cleaning the stairs.

Act 1, Scene 2

Act 1, Scene 2 introduces other family members: Alec, Isa and Jenny. Read the scene and note down any observations you have on the interplay between these characters and others we have met. For example: 'Alec: drunkenly aggressive towards John, conflict between them. Maggie defends him.'

If you have not read the rest of the play, can you predict how these relationships will develop?

- Alec and Isa
- Alec and John
- Alec and Maggie
- John and Jenny

Discussion

A tin of beans causes huge excitement in the Morrison family. What does this show us? Find three other references to food from anywhere in the scene and explain their importance.

Act 2

Act 2 starts a week after Act 1 and takes place over a month. It involves a series of comings and goings as tensions in the household increase:

- Alec and Isa are established so Granny has to go earlier to Lizzie's.

- Maggie returns from hospital but Bertie has been kept in.

- Jenny moves out.

- Isa threatens to leave Alec.

Spotlight on ... The neighbours as a Greek chorus

In ancient Greek drama, the 'chorus' was a group of characters who did not function as individuals but as a collective 'voice', providing moral or dramatic comment on the behaviour and personalities of the characters. They tended to be dressed the same, often wearing masks, and chanting or singing the same lines. They provided another, less personal, perspective on the action of the play. The group of neighbours can be seen as a modern version of the Greek chorus. Can you see similarities in the function they perform in *Men Should Weep*? In what ways are they different?

With a partner

At the end of Act 1, Maggie mentions the neighbours: we see how easy it is for them to fall out, living in such close proximity, but also how much the poor rely on each other to provide support of various sorts. At the beginning of Act 2, we see them in their glory. Looking at the opening of Act 2 (and thinking back to their appearance in Act 1), explain how the neighbours demonstrate or provide:

- malicious gossip
- good-hearted concern
- examples of theme, for example, domestic abuse
- homespun philosophy
- comfort and stability, for example, for a vulnerable character
- criticism of men – 'the enemy'.

Possible answers

Although they gain plenty of enjoyment from, for example, bringing home the latest story about Jenny, they also demonstrate genuine concern for one another, as in their concern for Maggie, Bertie, Mrs Bones and Granny. Mrs Bones is, of course, a victim of repeated domestic abuse: note that she never admits it (such things were accepted and not complained about openly). Comments such as 'When ye loss yer teeth, ye should loss yer appetite wi them' show a humorous, philosophical attitude, and there are many comments to Granny, for example, about how she will be missed. One thing that binds them together is their scorn for men as pathetic, feeble creatures: '... if their nebs is rinnin, they think they're deein'.

Spotlight on ... Lizzie – a real villain?

Although most of the characters in this play are a mixture of good and bad, like real people, Lizzie can be seen as a true villain. Where others are victims of poverty, she exploits the poverty of those around her. Even Alec and Isa, though selfish trouble makers, can be understood to an extent, but Lizzie has no real 'back story' to justify her hard, even cruel and malicious, behaviour. Right from her 'peremptory knock' (compare with Lily's 'brisk knock'), we can see that here is a demanding person, someone who is firmly focused on what she can get out of a situation. And yet, it is not that simple: she too has, to an extent, been moulded by poverty. Her harshness is perhaps her survival technique in a very difficult world.

With a partner or in small groups

Here is a series of quotations from Lizzie's only appearance in the play, in Act 2. Divide them up between you and explain what each one reveals about her.

1. (Ignoring the others – to Granny) 'Well? Ye ready?'
2. 'Got a yer claes packed? An yer pension book?'
3. 'Well, it's [the pension's] no Maggie's, it's mines. If ye're comin tae bide wi me, ye're no comin tae bide *aff* me.'
4. 'Folks that canna pay for their meat'll find nae room in ma hoose.'
5. 'Ye're jealous! Ye hevna the brains tae mak a bit yersels.'
6. 'Bide then!'
7. 'I'm sittin right here till Maggie comes hame wi whit's left o Granny's pension.'
8. (To Lily) 'Ye must hev an awfu nice boss ... Or mebbe you're awfu nice tae him, eh?'
9. 'Who says I'm no takin yon groceries?'
10. 'Sorry about the wean, Maggie. Ye should hae went up wi him afore.'

Possible answers

Quotations 1 and 5 show that Lizzie lacks basic courtesy to the neighbours and treats them with contempt.

Quotations 2, 3, 4, 7 and 9 are all about money and her desire to get it. Her suspicion is that other people are cheating her out of it.

In quotation 6, she shows no compassion or caring towards Granny.

In quotation 8, she is malicious-minded.

In quotation 10, she cannot help making nasty remarks, blaming Maggie for the severity of Bertie's illness. There may actually be some truth in what she says, but it is terribly cruel of her to say it.

Discussion

1. The neighbours clearly do not like or accept Lizzie. Why do you think this is?
2. When Maggie returns, why does Lizzie not press her for the pension money?
3. Why does Lizzie take Granny at all, considering she clearly does not want to?

Although the neighbours sometimes argue among themselves, they have a loyalty to one another and help each other out. Lizzie stands out as an exploiter of 'her own kind' (who has even committed fraud and been in prison for her illegal exploitation) and so is rejected by the group. They turn their backs on her (not that she cares). Notice that even hard, uncaring Lizzie cannot quite push the 'pension book' issue in the face of Maggie's extreme distress and she 'has to take her turn' of looking after Granny: there are unwritten rules which even she cannot break.

The end of Act 2, Scene 1 sees Maggie hit with the double blow of losing both Bertie (kept in hospital: his persistent cough is actually tuberculosis, a common killer in the 1930s) and Jenny (leaving home).

Spotlight on ... Jenny

Jenny's action in leaving home, when her mother is clearly devastated by Bertie's illness, seems heartless. In a way, it is. Yet we can also see her point of view. The flat is overcrowded; the close dirty and embarrassing. She is humiliated by her mother turning up begging for damaged foods at the shop. Her dressing up, dyeing her hair, wearing make-up – seen as 'tarty' – show her longing for the glamour so missing from her life. Note John's reaction in Act 1: scrubbing her face to remove the offensive make-up. Although a woman (in her own eyes), she is still treated as a child and the money she earns is not her own but put into the family funds. She is desperate to escape from a life of dirt and drudgery. But what does she escape to? Is Jenny at the end, though happier, any more in charge of her own destiny than her mother or grandmother?

Now, based on your knowledge so far, try these Scottish Text-type analysis questions.

Scottish Text questions

Read from 'I dinna ken whit wey ...' to 'I'm cryin for Jenny' in Act 2, Scene 1.

1. How does Lamont Stewart use stage directions to convey the relationship between Maggie and Alec? **2**
2. Analyse how the writer uses language to convey Jenny's feelings about leaving home. **4**
3. Analyse how language is used to contrast Maggie's and John's attitudes to Bertie's situation. **4**
4. By referring to this extract and elsewhere in the play, discuss how parent–child relationships are explored in the play. **10**

Possible answers

1. 'He smooths her hair ... her cheek' – a rare gesture of affection from Alec provokes Maggie to look 'gratefully' at him – she is so thankful that he is showing her tenderness. It is an undemonstrative world, but she 'lays his hand to her cheek', a gesture full of unspoken devotion and trust.

   'Alec disengages himself from his mother and grins feebly' – he is embarrassed to be 'caught' by Isa showing affection to his mother. In the face of her scorn, his mother's deep love for him is not important any more.

   2 marks for a detailed/insightful comment plus a quotation/reference. 1 mark for a more basic comment plus a quotation/reference. 0 marks for a quotation with no comment. Total: 2 marks. (Marks can be gained 2 or 1+1.)

2. 'Well, I'm awa. Cheeribye, everybody' – her lively cheerfulness shows her eagerness to be away, amounting to heartlessness in the context of Maggie's misery about Bertie and also about her leaving.

   'If they've [the neighbours] got the impidence tae ask, tell them it's nane o their bloomin business' – expressions like 'impidence' and 'nane o their bloomin business' suggest defiance for what 'the world' thinks. By implication, she is also defying Maggie – none of her business either.

   'I'm no in the mood for kissin' – her breezily callous refusal to show love for Maggie and dismissive attitude to her mother's love (which will later be so important).

   2 marks for a detailed/insightful comment plus a quotation/reference. 1 mark for a more basic comment plus a quotation/reference. 0 marks for a quotation with no comment. Total: 4 marks. (Marks can be gained 2+2, 2+1+1 or 1+1+1+1.)

3. Maggie: 'John they've kept him in' – a short, dramatic statement that reveals her stunned, pained reaction; 'I didna want ...' – repetition emphasises her pain; 'He'll be feart! He'll be cryin for his mammy!' – conjures up a painful picture of little Bertie, scared and alone, and shows her imaginative focus on her sick son.

   John: 'but it's better, Maggie, it's better' – repetition, reassuring/comforting her; focusing not on the pain of now but, rationally, on being sensible about what is best.

   'He'll be cryin ... cryin for Jenny' – slightly selfish; focus on his own pain, not that of his child.

   2 marks for a detailed/insightful comment plus a quotation/reference. 1 mark for a more basic comment plus a quotation/reference. 0 marks for a quotation with no comment. Total: 4 marks. (Marks can be gained 2+2, 2+1+1 or 1+1+1+1.)

4. **Up to 2 marks for a general explanation of how parent–child relationships are dealt with in the play (commonality). For example:**

   Love in such relationships is deep but not always expressed in a positive, simple way. Children can be manipulative, cruel and dismissive, though needy. Parents can be despairing, desperate, angry. Relationships are not always resolved.

   Up to 2 marks for comments on this section. For example:

   Maggie is so glad because she is unused to receiving a tangible demonstration of affection from Alec; She cannot understand Jenny's 'heartlessness' in leaving in this way; She is devastated by Bertie being kept in hospital; Neither Alec nor Jenny shows appreciation for these deep feelings: Alec is embarrassed; Jenny is focused on her own adventure.

   3 x 2 marks for comments and references from elsewhere in the play, of which there are many. Here are some examples:

   - John and Jenny: John is fiercely protective of Jenny and equally fiercely critical of her: for example, scrubbing the make-up off her face, dragging her in from the close when she is with a man.
   - Maggie and Jenny: Maggie longs for Jenny's return and is, ultimately, prepared to side with her in her efforts to support the family.
   - Maggie and Alec: Alec exploits Maggie's devotion to him, taking money from her and manipulating her to gain sympathy.   **Total: 10 marks.**

Remember that there are different ways of gaining full marks – your answers might be different from your friend's, but they might both be correct. This is particularly true of the final, 10-mark, question.

Act 2

This part of the play, and especially Scene 2, is dominated by the interplay of the two married couples in the family. There are six relationships going on simultaneously, each with its own issues. Put them all together and it's no wonder that tensions build and tempers fly!

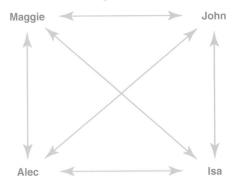

With a partner or in small groups

Select one, two or three of the six relationships and prepare a short presentation on its key aspects (aim for at least three). Think about, for example, how each person feels about the other (these will not necessarily be the same: for example, Alec's feelings for Isa and hers for him), how each behaves, whether one person is dominant in the relationship. Get together with another pair or group to share ideas. Alternatively, your group could present your findings on one or more relationship to the whole class.

Possible answers

Maggie and John

- The central relationship of the play, their warmth and genuine love for each other is one of the main positive elements in the play. Maggie says that, without this, she could not cope with the awful struggles of life.
- However, there are tensions. John clearly does not help Maggie much around the house, although he seems concerned about how exhausted she is. He even criticises the mess in the house in Act 2, Scene 2, although he could have tidied it while Maggie has been working.
- After flirting with Isa, John then defends her against Maggie's criticism – perhaps an even greater betrayal. He is certainly flawed and not fully appreciative of Maggie, even though his deeper feelings are for her.

Alec and Isa

- In contrast with Maggie and John, this relationship is mutually destructive and impacts negatively on others. They have brought chaos into the already strained Morrison household.
- Isa taunts Alec with her infidelity and her perception of him as useless, weak and unmanly.
- Alec veers between needy begging for attention and violent threats. Neither approach earns Isa's respect or love.

Maggie and Alec

- Of all her children, Alec is Maggie's favourite – despite being the least deserving of them all. She defends him against criticism from John and the scorn of Isa.
- The one time she has to face the truth, for a moment, is when she sees how much money he has taken from her purse.
- She tries to convince him of Isa's worthlessness, but he defends her and she is forced to accept this.

John and Alec

- John is critical of Alec: he does not see him through the positive, unconditionally loving eyes of Maggie.
- John is ashamed of Alec for making nothing of his life.
- Alec can be aggressive and resentful towards John.

Maggie and Isa

- Perhaps inevitably, as a spin-off of her devotion to Alec, Maggie is very critical of Isa.
- She sees her as a 'bad lot' and has absolutely no sympathy with her or sense that Alec might have contributed to their misfortunes.
- Isa hates Maggie and enjoys undermining the trust between her and John.

John and Isa

- In a short but significant betrayal, John flirts with Isa behind Maggie's back. He does not start it, but he allows it to happen – although he is ashamed afterwards.
- Isa delights in attracting John: she has so much resentment built up against Alec and Maggie. Is this a way of getting back at them? Remember also that John is a 'big, handsome man'.
- Isa forms a bond with John by laughing at Alec (and Maggie) with him. People who share a secret are closer!

Act 3

In Act 3, two aspects are particularly significant:

- the contrast in atmosphere at the start of this act – much lighter, happier and more positive
- the way the various plot strands and character developments come together to create the climax of the play.

In small groups

In this task you are going to analyse the opening of Act 3 (up to Lily's arrival). Consider the following features, this time making comparisons with the opening of Act 1:

- setting
- stage directions
- plot
- character development
- thematic development.

Each person in the group should take one or two features of the opening of Act 3 and note down his or her impressions. Then get together to share your ideas. When we compare the openings of Acts 1 and 3, what do we notice?

Possible answers

- **Setting:** it is the same room, but transformed. Through the money from John's new job, not only is there a sense of festivity and prosperity – 'decorations, vase of paper flowers' – but it is also 'clean, tidy', as if, suddenly, the chaos that went along with poverty has gone. We see Ernest with the much-desired football boots and radio – his dreams fulfilled.
- **Stage directions:** Ernest playing football, Granny smiling, Maggie polishing 'her few bits of brassware' – the kind of non-essential household task she now has time to do. John is smartly dressed, 'happy and confident': finally he has pride in himself as the provider. The red hat is, of course, symbolic: it is frivolous, not just 'functional', and similar to one Maggie had in their 'coortin' days. By giving her this, he is trying to return to those early romantic times. Maggie's obvious pleasure shows how effective it is. When the neighbours arrive, instead of bread and jeely, they eat Christmas cake and chocolate biscuits.
- **Plot:** it is Christmas Eve. John arrives home to take Ernest shopping for a ball (to go with the boots), having already bought Maggie the hat: she is his priority. Granny's criticism of the hat as 'nae a colour for an aul wife' does not dampen the mood. The neighbours gather for convivial tea and cake. The symbolism of the hat is clear again: it prompts the neighbours to remember their days of happiness before marriage and poverty took it away.
- **Character development:** like the setting, the characters are transformed. Maggie and John are celebratory, the warmth of their love finding a more overt and happy expression. The squabbling and complaining – which is still going on – is the kind found in 'normal' families: Maggie and Ernest disagree about music; Granny complains about Ernest playing noisily. If the play ended here, it would seem they had all found their happy endings, but it does not. The mention of Alec and Isa 'clouds' Maggie's 'happy face'.
- **Thematic development:** that a simple thing like a modest wage can bring such happiness is a social comment in itself. Of course, John's money will not solve the deeper issues, such as Bertie's illness and the family/marital breakup. And Maggie's heroism is still to be tested further ...

Task

On your own or with a partner

To establish an overview of this crucial act, here is a breakdown of the key events. Try to find a quotation for each stage, to familiarise yourself with key moments and their significance.

A. Convivial, harmonious atmosphere with Maggie, Granny, Lily and the neighbours sharing chat and Christmas cake.

B. Disrupted by arrival of Alec, who is rude and unpleasant – and looking for Isa.

C. Lily encourages Maggie to go shopping – the first time we see Maggie do anything 'just for herself'.

D. Return of Isa, leading to a violent confrontation between her and Alec.

E. Maggie returns to the scene of the fight and becomes upset. Lily is comforting.

F. Jenny returns: revelation about Bertie, reconciliation with Maggie, and Lily's scornful commentary in the background.

G. Arrival of John and confrontation with Jenny.

H. Maggie asserts herself and humiliates John.

I. Hopeful ending.

Some of these stages are longer than others: (A), for example, is several pages; (I) is just a few lines. However, each is an important element in the climax of the play. There are many possible appropriate quotations. Get together in a group to share your ideas.

Let's look in detail at the various plot/character strands. First of all, we will establish what these are:

- Alec and Isa's story of marital conflict

- Jenny's story – the desire for independence

- Bertie's illness – can he come home? (Note that Bertie never actually appears in the play, yet he is an important character. Consider why this is.)

- Maggie and John – will he find work and will her struggles pay off?

Although there are other 'stories' in the play, such as what will happen to Granny, these four are the ones that have a definite progression towards an ending – even if the ending is not fully resolved. They each have an impact on the play's eventual outcome.

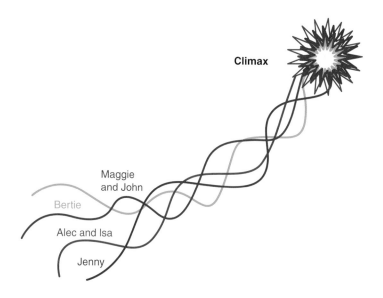

Climax

Maggie and John

Bertie

Alec and Isa

Jenny

With a partner

Choose one of the main plot strands and:

- briefly trace its progress through the play
- in more detail, examine how it reaches a climax in Act 3. You can use your answers for the task on page 17 as a starting point and build on these.

Possible answers

Maggie and John

Act 1: Although they love each other, there are tensions related to John's lack of a job and their resulting poverty. John resents the interference and criticism of Lily and is not keen on allowing Alec and Isa to move in (unlike Maggie). Maggie attempts to hide from John the fact that Jenny is out late, but cannot prevent his outburst when Jenny arrives.

Act 2: As things fall apart, John and Maggie continue to struggle to support each other. The loss of Jenny and Bertie leaves Maggie distraught and John full of self-accusation and despair. John allows himself to be drawn into flirting with Isa and laughing at Maggie and Alec behind Maggie's back. He is ashamed when Maggie returns, exhausted and starving. Maggie loses control when John sides with Isa and he comforts her with tenderness.

Act 3: The scene begins on a positive, harmonious and happy note. John, now employed, has regained his self-respect and takes delight in giving Maggie the red hat for Christmas. He arrives home (from shopping) to find Jenny urging Maggie to accept the money she has saved to rent a proper, healthy house for Bertie to come home to. John refuses to accept Jenny's 'whore's winnins', shocking Maggie with this coarse and hateful expression. It is not his pride (he would have gladly taken the money if she had earned it 'respectably') but the shame of her 'living in sin' and taking money from her lover.

Faced with the choice between reconciliation with Jenny and Bertie's return – or supporting John (as she has done throughout the play) – Maggie asserts herself and takes the money. She exposes John's hypocrisy in condemning Jenny by revealing intimate details of their pre-marital relationship ('Whit wis I, when we were coortin, but your tart?'). She humiliates him by accusing him of lusting after Isa ('the way ye looked at yer ain son's wife trailing aboot the hoose wi her breasts fa'in oot o her fancy claes') and, in a chilling moment, reminding him of his furtive, desperate seduction of her years before ('Maggie! Come on, quick, ben the back room ... lock the door ... it'll no tak minutes ...'). She immediately regrets exposing their private life in this way ('There's things atween husbands an wives shouldna be spoke aboot') while John, ashamed of himself, allows Jenny to take his hand. A traumatic but hopeful moment, as Maggie hopes 'There'll be flowers come the spring!'

Scottish Text questions

These analysis questions are based on a section of Act 3, starting from when Maggie arrives back (from going after Alec) and ending with Lily and Maggie going shopping, from 'Maggie: Whit about Jenny?' to 'Lily: ... *Come on!*'

1. Look at the opening lines of this section: from 'Maggie: Aye. She paid for the dressin' to '... whit wey they turn oot.' Analyse how language is used to show the contrasting attitudes of Maggie and Lily towards Jenny. **4**
2. The neighbours discuss their husbands. Identify the contrast between the way they talk about marriage and the way they behave towards their husbands. **2**
3. Much of this section involves Maggie and Lily talking to, or about, Granny. By referring to the dialogue and/or stage directions in this section, explain Granny's own attitudes to life and the attitudes Maggie and Lily demonstrate towards her. **4**
4. By referring to this section and elsewhere in the play, discuss how the relationship between Maggie and Lily is developed. **10**

Possible answers

1. **Maggie:** admiring towards Jenny, longing for her: 'Whiles I dream aboot her ... pop in on me.' Attempting to sound light and less distraught: 'pop in'. Depth of her love for Jenny expressed in: 'Once they've been laid ... turn oot'. The physical and lifelong connection between mother and child emphasised.

   Lily: matter-of-fact, unsentimental: 'She said she wouldnae come back ... no comin back.' Repetition of sentence structure hammers home certainty that she will not return.

   2 marks for a detailed/insightful comment plus a quotation/reference. 1 mark for a more basic comment plus a quotation/reference. 0 marks for a quotation with no comment. Total: 4 marks. (Marks can be gained 2+2, 2+1+1 or 1+1+1+1.)

2. The women speak scornfully and dismissively about their husbands (**1 mark**) but still do as they are told/husbands are still in charge (**1 mark**). **Total: 2 marks.**

3. Granny: has no control over her own life/cannot make decisions even about basic things like when she goes to bed/her only way of asserting herself is to complain constantly and impotently/knows they are 'up to something'. Plus quotation/reference.

   Maggie and Lily: good-humoured (and in Maggie's case, warm) but no-nonsense control of Granny. She is put to bed, out of the way, when her presence is inconvenient. They treat her like a child, offering sweets, etc. Plus quotation/reference.

   2 marks for a detailed/insightful comment plus a quotation/reference. 1 mark for a more basic comment plus a quotation/reference. 0 marks for a quotation with no comment. Total: 4 marks. (Marks can be gained 2+2, 2+1+1 or 1+1+1+1.)

4. **Up to 2 marks for a general explanation of Maggie and Lily's relationship in the play (commonality). For example:**

   Explanation of how Lily and Maggie's relationship develops: although they differ and disagree, they do have a close bond. Lily genuinely wants the best for Maggie, who does appreciate her help. They move from Lily criticising Maggie to admiring/supporting her at the end.

   Up to 2 marks for comments on this section. For example:

   Lily does not understand Maggie's need to believe that Jenny will return and cannot grasp the depth of emotion between mother and child; Lily urges Maggie to go shopping/to enjoy something 'for herself'; Maggie thanks Lily for constant help with family; Lily comes close to telling Maggie she loves her.

   3 x 2 marks for comments and references from elsewhere in the play, of which there are many. Here are some examples:

   - Lily is irritated by Maggie's inability to sort out the muddle of the family's life – reference to Act 1.
   - Nonetheless, she offers Maggie practical help, for example the tin of beans (and many other similar gifts).
   - Lily does not (immediately) tell Maggie that Alec owes her money – she tries to protect her from this upsetting news.   **Total: 10 marks.**

Finally, a touch of humour. *Men Should Weep* could be a dismal, depressing drama. Obviously there is a lot of suffering in the play and the outcome is, at best, hopeful rather than resolved. However, it is far from miserable. This is partly because of Maggie herself: as a symbol for the determination and resilience of the human spirit, she provides a dash of hope. Another reason for the richness of the play's appeal is the humour, which is often dark – a coping mechanism in difficult times. It is a very funny play!

Task

With a partner or in small groups

As a final, lighter task, try to find five examples of humour in the play. These could be funny dialogue or the shocked reaction of a character, based on a situation. Try to find as varied a mixture as you can, involving as many characters as possible. You could start with:

Granny: Ma lif's ebbin. Ebbin awa.

Maggie: Och, it's been ebbin ever since I met ye; but the tide aye seems tae come in again.

PROSE NOVEL: *SUNSET SONG*

BY LEWIS GRASSIC GIBBON

Sunset Song is a powerful and evocative novel, rediscovered by generation after generation since first emerging in 1932. It deals with potential, promise, loss and, above all, change and how we, as human beings, deal with it. To do this, the novel draws its readers into a fictionalised version of the world its author, Lewis Grassic Gibbon, grew up in. He left, keen to sample the bigger world beyond, in his teens – and on revisiting years later was startled into writing by the great changes he now saw. His visit home reminded him of why he loved – and had sometimes hated – the way of life in the Mearns of Angus.

The story he constructed is that of a girl growing into womanhood in what was, in 1911, a traditional crofting family – renting out and working a small, mixed farm. The family moves home in 'Ploughing' (Chapter 1) from Aberdeenshire into Grassic Gibbon's own, slightly more southern, territory of the Mearns. Their new 'parish' of Kinraddie – kirk (church) and crofting homesteads spread around a few square miles – corresponded to Grassic Gibbon's real parish of Arbuthnott.

When reading the novel it is a good idea to start with 'Ploughing': the American edition included a note from Grassic Gibbon himself advising this.

You may work through this book while reading the novel section by section, or read the whole novel before beginning. This book is designed to allow either approach. The next few pages will provide an overview of characters, main events and thematic development. If you want to avoid any 'spoilers', look at these pages later.

Characters

Obviously, this is Chris's novel. In the diagram on the right, the other characters are arranged around her, with the 'formative' influences on her at the bottom and the characters who are important later nearer the top. You will see that some names are larger than others: this reflects how important they are to Chris's development (although they all matter).

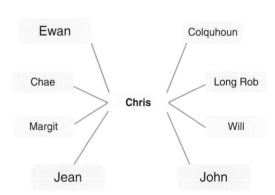

Task

With a partner

Choose two characters from the diagram above, one large and one small. List the ways they impact on Chris's life and development.

Overview

Here is a brief summary of the major events in the main sections of the novel.

With a partner or in small groups

1. For 'Ploughing' and 'Drilling', work out the significance of each major event for Chris's development as a character. The first two have been done for you. Note that this could be done as a revision exercise when you have read and studied the whole novel.

'Ploughing'

Event	Significance
Birth of twins (at Echt)	Chris is horrified by her mother's suffering. Learns about sex
Move to Blawearie	Chris feels a connection with standing stones and the past
Father's violence towards Will	
Friendship with Margit	
Washing the clothes	
Mother becomes withdrawn and worried	

'Drilling'

Event	Significance
Mother's death	
Threshing at Peesie's Napp. Community gossip about Chris	
Fire at Chae's. Ewan kisses Chris	
Father is injured	

2. For 'Seed-time', this time work out which major events have significance for Chris.

'Seed-time'

Event	Significance
	At first relief, then grief as love is renewed
	Independent – chooses to stay on the land rather than leaving to study
	Realisation of passionate love for Ewan
	Day of personal happiness and community support
	Fears and uncertainty as a 'third Chris' replaces her old self

3. Finally, for 'Harvest', choose five significant events and state their significance for Chris as she grows to mature womanhood. One has been done to start you off.

'Harvest'

Event	Significance
Birth of young Ewan	Perfect happiness and fulfilment in their little family

Themes

The diagrams below give a breakdown of two important themes in *Sunset Song*: love of the land and change. Breaking down a theme in this way is an effective way of building your knowledge and confidence, whichever novel you are studying.

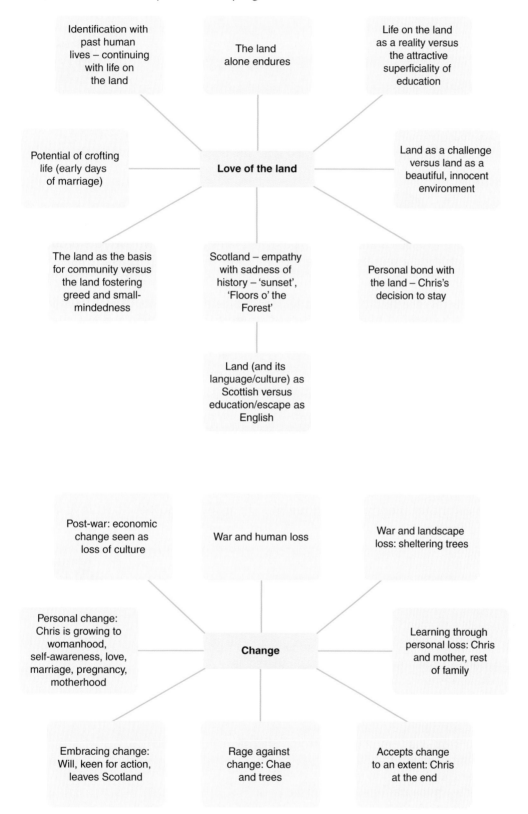

'Ploughing'

Let's begin by looking closely at the opening of 'Ploughing', bearing in mind the key strands of character, setting and theme. This chapter is about character introduction, gently done by placing Chris in a landscape, therefore letting character interact with setting. Read from 'Below and around where Chris Guthrie lay ...' to 'drooped red and rusty already'.

Task

With a partner

1. The hilltop moorland scenery is 'below and around' her. She is central and we know she is responsive to her surroundings. Which word choice groupings suggest this and what do they imply about her?
2. How does Grassic Gibbon make it clear that Chris is the observer?
3. In what way does the description change topic and tone in the paragraph's second half?

Possible answers

1. Choices could include 'whispered and rustled', 'powdered faintly' and 'brave with the beauty of it'. They all imply an intimacy, a sensitivity to details, which we attach to Chris as the human being lying there, looking and listening.

2. Look at this extract from the second sentence: '... and maybe the wind would veer there in an hour or so and you'd feel the change in the life and strum of the thing, bringing in a streaming coolness out of the sea'. That switch to the second person 'you' brings us very close to Chris's thoughts as she yearns for a change in the weather. It is the 'you' that we might use in talking about a personal experience. The novel has no first-person narrative, but Grassic Gibbon uses various ways to bring us close to the workings of Chris's mind.

3. It turns to more practical matters, is more down-to-earth, even slightly ominous perhaps – although Chris does not appear overly concerned personally with the drought-stricken hay and potatoes of the farm's 'parks'. There is no clear break, though, and we see a tension between what is beautiful and lyrical and what is useful and life-preserving.

Let's establish a framework for the whole of 'Ploughing', focusing on how the narrative links to character, setting and theme.

Task

With a partner

Here is a list of narrative moments:

1. Chris on the hill, thinking of weather and local folk.
2. Family background – Chris's memories and her mother's tales.
3. Chris and education – realisation of 'the two Chrisses'.
4. Birth of the twins.
5. Leaving Aberdeenshire and journeying to the Mearns (through the storm).
6. Early days in the new farm of Blawearie.
7. The college at Duncairn and friendship with Margit Strachan.
8. Andy's 'scandalous rampage'.
9. The election of Reverend Gibbon as minister.
10. Chris and mother wash the blankets.
11. Back to the storytelling 'present' on the hillside – Dod and Alec appear, running up to Chris.

The story does not just exist by itself: it is used to develop other aspects. With your partner, having read the list of key strands below, decide which elements of the novel are involved in the narrative moments above. Remember that there may be more than one letter for each number; such overlap is inevitable in a complex text like this.

A. Character creation.
B. Interplay between characters.
C. Significant events.
D. Setting.
E. Character and setting interaction.

Narrative moment	1	2	3	4	5	6	7	8	9	10	11
Key strand											

Possible answers

Narrative moment	1	2	3	4	5	6	7	8	9	10	11
Key strand	A, E	A, B, C	A, E	A, B, C	C, D, E	B, E	A, B	A, B, E	A, B, C, E	B, C	B, C, E

Spotlight on ... Theme – changing life in Scotland

Grassic Gibbon did not set out to write a tale about the captivating doings of couthy country folk. He had points to make: this novel is theme-driven. One of his points is that crofting life was not like its portrayal in the sentimental 'Kailyard' writing that had dominated Scottish countryside fiction for the previous 50 years. His desire for realism made him enemies in his own boyhood home.

Grassic Gibbon's unique style has, without a doubt, been a major factor in the ongoing popularity of this novel. We will look now at what makes it quite different and distinctive.

Style 1: Chris's perspective

We have already looked at this in the opening of the novel, so now for a closer examination of other moments from 'Ploughing'.

> So Will hated father, he was sixteen years of age and near a man, but father could still make him cry like a bairn. He would whisper his hate to Chris as they lay in their beds at night in the loft room high in the house and the harvest moon came sailing over the Barmekin and the peewits wheeped above the lands of Echt. And Chris would cover her ears and then listen, turning this cheek to the pillow and that, she hated also and she didn't hate, father, the land, the life of the land – oh, if only she knew!

One thing you may have noticed is the use of sentence structure to provide a continuous, almost hypnotic rhythmic flow. This is achieved by the use of the link words common in oral, spoken, storytelling, such as 'so', 'and' and 'but'. These often appear at the start of sentences and proliferate within them. Commas are frequently used where full stops would be grammatically correct. The flow is the main thing.

The 'and' linkage makes the descriptions of harvest moon and peewits seem as important as that of Will's resentful whisperings and Chris's initial reactions. We are left with a sense that the combination of human life and nature provides Chris with reassurance and comfort. Complicated family life is counterbalanced by finding something simpler, and more dependable, in nature.

The flow is disrupted in the second half of the last sentence, and because this is such a contrast, it is very noticeable. Chris is having to deal with family conflict and her own inner conflict. The style is broken and dramatic, especially at the very end: '– oh, if only she knew!'

However, the simple language and use of repetition resonates with what has gone before. The style varies but is consistent; and Grassic Gibbon maintains this consistency of storytelling, narrative 'voice' throughout.

Read the section from: 'So that was Chris and her ready ...' to '... worth the saying at all.' This is one of the novel's best-liked, most-quoted passages. It goes to the heart of what Grassic Gibbon sees in Chris – and saw in himself in the culture and life of his boyhood. However, it also shows us the cultural paradox that Scotland was in as he wrote the novel, and the choices, it seemed, it would have to make: be true to tradition and to cultural identity, or put this by to focus on the present and the future.

On your own or with a partner

1. Show in detail how Grassic Gibbon's style of writing takes us in close to the back-and-forth conflict within Chris's mind.
2. Explain clearly the dilemma she faces.

Possible answers

1. 'two Chrisses' – the idea of two extremes competing within her.

   Word choice 'fought', 'tormented' – shows the real strain she is under in trying to choose.

   Juxtaposition of feelings: 'You hated the land ... one day; the next ... And the next ... for a while ...'. We are shown her feelings switching back and forward, back and forward.

   We see her love of the 'sweetness of the land', of the 'faces dear and close to you' and of Scots words, opposed by lists of reasons for preferring an English education.

2. She can take the route of education, most likely ending up in the respectable profession of teacher, but separated from the countryside and her Scottish roots.

   Alternatively, she can stay on the land but be aware of the physical hardship and limitations of living here.

   Later she will find herself to some degree independent, and able to choose of her own free will, making a crucial decision.

Style 2: The narrative 'voice' of the community

When Andy, 'the daftie', does his wild run through the fields and woods, the narrative voice draws away from Chris for this community gossip, with its own particular mix of sarcastic humour, nosy curiosity and indignation.

Read from 'When sight of the Mains ...' to '... Have you seen that creature Andy?' Here, descriptive word and phrase choices ('the futret' [ferret]/'go sleeking down'/'sharp as you like') sketch a derogatory picture of Mistress Munro before we see her in action, accusing everyone else of helping in Andy's 'escape'.

The tendency of people to criticise, mock and generally pass judgement on each other is made clear throughout the novel. This often critical, sometimes small-minded, prejudiced and hypocritical community voice will later be turned against Chris herself, making a clear separation from the empathetic, intimate use to which the narrative voice is more often put. Even so, the style remains *consistent*: we have a sense of the fluidity of speech, of thought.

With a partner

Choose another moment in 'Ploughing' and analyse Grassic Gibbon's style of presenting narrative and character. You might select, for example, the birth of the twins, Will's use of the word 'Jehovah' or Chris's visit to the manse to collect a book from the Reverend Gibbon.

Style 3: The Scots language

Just as Chris faced a difficult choice regarding being 'Scottish' and 'English', so Grassic Gibbon faced the dilemma of how to convey the sense of a Scots-speaking community in English, for an international readership. His choice was to write in 'Scots-enriched English', using many Scots words 'straight' (for example, 'bucht', 'futret' and 'gowked') or in slightly 'Anglicised' forms (for example, 'braw' becomes 'brave' and 'chiel' becomes 'childe'). This use of language helps create a sense of place and identity, and also perhaps of change, as there is a strong sense of English as the coming language, the one needed to 'get ahead'. Scots can be grouped with the trees (lamented by Chae), and the men slain in battle, as part of Grassic Gibbon's vision of an older Scotland passing – and yet this novel has updated Scots' credentials, showing how immediate and effective a language it remains.

Spotlight on ... Jean Guthrie

A compelling character emotionally, if only seen in fleeting glimpses. Look at her as a contrast to John, her blithe bonniness and natural joy in life ever-weakening in the grip of his increasing harshness; also as an influence on Chris (her happy memory of barefoot childhood days tramping country roads or working in the fields resonates through the novel). Her 'moments' are often dramatic: childbirth; failed attempts to intercede on Will's or Chris's behalf with John; her suicide and murder of the twins. Contrast the tortured sexuality of her marriage with the natural passion of Chris's relationship with Ewan.

'Drilling'

Confident knowledge of 'Drilling' can be achieved by focusing on two things:

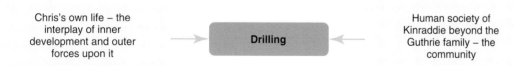

In Chris's life we can see two strands:

- the narrowing down of life as she suffers repeated loss, both of people and of life opportunities
- the awakening of her sense of self as she matures from girlhood to womanhood.

Task

With a partner

Identify aspects of Chris's experience that contribute to both 'strands' of her development as a character. Aim for three examples of each, though find more if you can.

Narrowing down	Awakening/developing

Possible answers

Narrowing down	Awakening/developing
Death of mother and the twins – a sense that part of her is gone forever	Awareness of self, following the tink's comments
John Guthrie padding around, trying her door	Awareness of the joy of running across fields
Constant labour in the kitchen or the field	Excitement after stolen kiss
Will leaving – alone with John Guthrie	Awareness of her physical response to Ewan

Setting

What we learn about Kinraddie's community and see in Chris's reaction to it echoes the author's own conflicted viewpoint of his Mearns upbringing. There is much that is small-minded and stifling, but there is something to warm to and love.

Task

With a partner

Find positive and negative examples of the community's role or influence in this chapter. This is an activity that can be repeated for other chapters throughout the novel.

Positive	Negative
Genuine pleasure at news of minister's baby	Signs that the Guthrie family tragedy is seen as shameful

Possible answers

Positive	Negative
Genuine pleasure at news of minister's baby	Signs that the Guthrie family tragedy is seen as shameful
Chae and Rob's open minds at threshing	Pleasure at Chris giving up education
Community action at fire	Malicious gossip regarding Will and Mollie
Chae and Rob visiting at New Year	More gossip when Will leaves

Scottish Text questions

The community has gathered to help with the December threshing of corn at Chae Strachan's farm. The men thresh; the women prepare and serve food. Read from 'The first three men ...' to 'night star coming in the sky', then try these analysis questions.

1. Analyse the opening paragraph and first sentence of the second paragraph to demonstrate how Chris's negative feelings begin and build up.   **4**
2. Explain why the final sentence of the second paragraph is very effective in showing Chris's change of heart.   **2**
3. What differing aspects of Chris's character are we made aware of in her reaction to Ewan Tavendale?   **2**
4. How does Grassic Gibbon remind us of, and bring to life, another aspect of Chris's character in the final paragraph?   **2**

You should be able to answer the final question fully if you have read the whole novel. If not, note down as many ideas as you can from what you have read so far.

5. By referring to this extract and elsewhere in the novel, discuss Chris's relationship with the community.   **10**

Possible answers

1. Picture of Chris working hard juxtaposed with the description of Mutch greedily attacking the soup – only a cursory word in Chris's direction.

   'a spree to the pair of them' suggests Chris thinks they're just there for the food.

   As she works, she hears Munro's patronising, diminishing comments.

   Culminates in loathing/scorn for the limitations of all men there.

   2 marks for a detailed/insightful comment plus a quotation/reference. 1 mark for a more basic comment plus a quotation/reference. 0 marks for a quotation with no comment. Total: 4 marks. (Marks can be gained 2+2, 2+1+1 or 1+1+1+1.)

2. It shows Chris's sudden awareness that she has over-generalised (**1 mark**). It draws attention to the thoughtfulness possible in the most humble, uneducated folk (**1 mark**). **Total: 2 marks.**

3. Instinctive, emotional, uncertain, learning about life (**1 mark**). Cool, composed, self-sufficient, self-aware (**1 mark**). **Total: 2 marks.**

4. Her feeling of physical closeness to/affection for the countryside. We are shown her sense of physical well-being from being out in/observing nature. Plus quotation/reference.

   2 marks for a detailed/insightful comment plus a quotation/reference. 1 mark for a more basic comment plus a quotation/reference. 0 marks for a quotation with no comment. Total: 2 marks. (Marks can be gained 2 or 1+1.)

5. **Up to 2 marks for general explanation of Chris's relationship with the community (commonality).**

   Chris often finds herself torn between contempt for the community's small-mindedness and a strong sense of identification with it.

   Up to 2 marks for discussing her relationship with the community, as shown by this extract.

   She is appalled by the way the men of the community seek to reduce women to kitchen servants, but has a sudden insight into the worth of Long Rob and Chae.

3 x 2 marks for comments and references from elsewhere in the novel, of which there are many. Here are some examples:

- Guthrie's funeral: Chris is overwhelmed by grief at the graveside – this 'softens' the community's view of her, which had been critical before.
- Chris's wedding: overall feeling of shared emotion, exemplified by Old Pooty and his present and the kindly-meant advice of Mistress Mutch.
- After Ewan's death: Chris outrages the women of the community by her hostility towards their platitudes. **Total: 10 marks.**

On your own or with a partner

Put together a 10-mark answer on Chris's love of the land. Again, this is only possible if you are already familiar with the rest of the novel. If not, come back to it later. Remember you are linking the sense of 'love of the land' which you find in the extract to its development elsewhere in the novel.

To help with organisation of your research, you may find this structure helpful:

(a) Chris's feelings for the land.
(b) How she acts on these feelings when she can.
(c) The land as solace and comfort.
(d) The land lost but forever in her heart.

Here are other aspects of Chris's character which you could consider for this sort of question:

- Chris growing to womanhood at a time of change.
- Chris's symbolic role – tradition and progress.
- Chris as a critic of her society.
- Chris – history and a sense of Scotland.

Spotlight on … John Guthrie

If Jean symbolises an innocence that pre-dates organised religion, John is the antithesis of this. A demanding, vengeful God, and the land as an enemy to be battled with, symbolise all that Grassic Gibbon deplored about the development of religion and society. Guthrie is trapped in a way of life and a mindset that warp him. When he loses his grim self-control after his stroke, he appears to grow disinhibited, becoming an unbearable tyrant – and, in a daringly realistic development by the author, incestuously inclined. And yet, there is kindness to animals, a belief in Chris's education, a respect for Chris and a fondness that the years of toil and bitterness have hidden.

'Seed-time'

As the novel's longest and most positive chapter, there is much to take from 'Seed-time' about the rich potential of the country way of life. The positive aspects of the human community come to a climax at Chris's wedding. This human landscape is an important part of the novel's setting – confident knowledge of this will certainly help in the exam.

On your own or with a partner

'Seed-time' begins with the death of John Guthrie. Explain why it is important (think of plot, character and symbolism). How do you account for Chris's sudden grief at the graveside?

Possible answers

This event is pivotal for plot: it sets Chris free (from John's 'enslavement' and also financially, thanks to his will). It is also important for characterisation, showing Chris's fundamental toughness and independence of spirit. We see her calm exhilaration at his passing and her equally calm, methodical business dealings afterwards. Symbolically, an older, dourer male-dominated Calvinist Scotland has been laid to rest, and a more youthful, rational, unprejudiced and more sexually balanced Scotland has emerged.

Chris's sudden grief at John's graveside is a powerful moment. Grassic Gibbon reveals the complexity of human relationships. Chris, though tough, is deeply emotional and fair (which we see developed in 'Harvest'). Her appreciation of her father's efforts on the family's behalf – along with the determined, practical aspect of her decision to take on the farm – help us to see her indebtedness to him.

Dunottar Castle, Stonehaven, Aberdeenshire

The wedding

On your own or with a partner

Read again from 'It came in snow that morning' to '... tea to waken Ewan and herself'.

1. Write down two examples of the more negative aspects of people's behaviour found here. (Bear in mind Grassic Gibbon's hatred of sentimentalism and idealising – his aim is a type of enhanced realism.)
2. The positives: what do the following examples add to our feeling that this community is worthwhile, a good place in human terms?
   (a) Pooty's arrival.
   (b) The atmosphere in the parlour as Chris arrives.
   (c) The dancing.
   (d) The singing.

Possible answers

1. **Negative aspects:**

   * The minister's behaviour with the 'maid from the Mearns' – a sense of the hypocrisy of religion in the community.
   * Mistress Munro's theft of cakes – the self-seeking that competes with community spirit.

2. **Positive aspects:**

   (a) Pooty's arrival:
   Link with a generous, sharing, though self-sufficient way of life (gift of handmade shoes).
   Effort he has put in to get there.
   The warmth and spontaneity this ignites in Chris in return.
   (b) The atmosphere in the parlour as Chris arrives:
   Quiet solemnity – respectfulness for significance of moment.
   Gentle, unassuming behaviour of Chae and the bridesmaids.
   The lovely words of the service.
   The sudden outbreak of cheerfulness and congratulations.
   (c) The dancing:
   Led by Chae and Rob, community's true moral 'heart'.
   Exuberance of dancing (contrast to harsh landscape outside).
   Interjections of considered, serious advice from Mistress Mutch, Chae and Rob.
   (d) The singing:
   The depth and poignancy of the sadder songs bring feeling of shared humanity.

Chris and Ewan on their croft

The early months of Chris and Ewan's life together flow naturally into the pregnancy, birth and parenthood section that begins 'Harvest'.

Task

With a partner

Read again from 'So that was her marriage ...' to 'let's get out and get off'.

1. In what way does this section show the potential and promise in the crofting life – which is not there, for example, in the marriages of John and Jean or Chae and Kirsty?
2. In what way does the trip to Edzell Castle reveal a certain distance between Chris and Ewan?
3. Explain the changing mental perspective that comes over Chris with her realisation that she is pregnant.
4. What does the incident of the slapping reveal about their relationship? Notice that the slapping is mutual: why is this important?

Possible answers

1. Even harsh winter mornings are pleasurable because of their love. The morning work routine is done in cheerful unison – different tasks but companionship/partnership; for example, he shoots rabbits and she sells them to grocer. Hard work constantly, but no complaining – good humour and affection win through. The only anger is Ewan's at Chris working too hard.

2. 'The remoteness that her books had made': Chris understands aspects of the castle of which Ewan is ignorant, and that heraldic beasts never actually existed. She has a sense of living history – of the folk who had once lived there – and is disappointed that they cannot share this.

3. She realises her carefree days have gone. She identifies with all the other women who have undergone this. She feels trapped and is (unreasonably) angry that Ewan does not share this burden.

4. There is potential for pride and fury (even violence), but it passes quickly. We see that they both play an active role in the conflict: Chris is not simply a victim.

Spotlight on ... Long Rob

With Chae, Hogmanay visitor to the bereaved Guthries, the champion of Chris at the Peesie's Knapp threshing and the wedding entertainment, Rob represents enlightenment in an often restrictive environment. He is keenly sceptical, accepting no pre-formed opinions or gossip. He seems to be an atheist, which is quite unusual in that community, and is prepared to suffer for his individual principles and views (especially during the war). He seems, at times, a loner, entirely self-sufficient, but this is not true, as we see, for example, after his return from prison. Just as his song rings out to Chris at key moments, so Chris helps him 'back to life'. It is Rob's independence of mind and spirit that sets him apart. He seems to symbolise the need for non-conformity, questioning and restless intelligence in any society.

'Harvest'

The closing chapter of the novel sees themes and narrative coming to fruition. The disruption caused by the war is followed by the climax of Ewan's death and the renewed love and reconciliation when Chris learns the truth.

Task

In small groups

Here is a list of narrative moments:

1. The Tavendales, living very happily on the farm.
2. Birth.
3. Anti-German feelings grow.
4. Rob defiant.
5. Chae and the woods.
6. Chae's vision of a chariot.
7. Ewan goes off to war.
8. Will visits, full of the better life abroad.
9. Chris supports Rob.
10. Ewan's terrible visit.
11. Chris losing herself in the harvest.
12. The affair with Rob.
13. Chris's reaction to news of Ewan's death.
14. Chae's true story of Ewan's execution.
15. Ewan's 'return' to Chris.

Match the narrative moments with the themes below. Some may recur several times; some will double or triple up. Remember that analysing complex literature can involve different readers holding different opinions, which could all be valid. The important thing is to be able to justify your views.

A. Change versus tradition in women's lives.
B. Change.
C. The importance of the land.
D. The potential of the crofting life.
E. Life as a battle with nature.
F. The effects of war.
G. Individual conscience versus community pressure.
H. The continuity of history.
I. An evaluation of where Scotland stands.
J. Positive and negative aspects of the community.
K. The place of love in times of crisis.

Narrative moment	1	2	3	4	5	6	7	8	9	10	11	12	13	14	15
Theme															

Possible answers

Narrative moment	1	2	3	4	5	6	7	8	9	10	11	12	13	14	15
Theme	C, D	A, E	F, G, J	F, G, J	B, C, E, F, I	H	F, G, H, K	B, I	F, G, I	A, F, K	C, F	A, C, F, K	A, F, G, I, K	A, C, F, G, K	C, K

Task

In small groups

In your groups, each person should pick one of the narrative moments in the previous task. Collect evidence to justify the choice of one or more themes. Get back together with your group to explain your ideas. Here is one example:

Narrative moment 7: Ewan goes off to war

Themes: F, G, H and K

Why choose H – 'the continuity of history'? One difference between Ewan and Chris is his lack of a sense of history. He has no interest in the war but, unlike Chris, with her knowledge of and strong feelings for the injustices suffered by people across the centuries, he has no strong standpoint either. His absorption in farm and family is no defence against the scornful accusations that he is cowardly and unpatriotic. Chris can see this war as the latest in a long line of disastrous decisions made by those in power, the 'rulers and gentry' she hated with 'John Guthrie's hate'.

The key theme: change

The novel deals with the effect of a time of dramatic turbulence on a traditional way of life. Grassic Gibbon develops the theme primarily in relation to the development of its central character whose life is influenced by large-scale historical change in various key ways. However, other characters are also used to illustrate this major theme.

Task

With a partner

Read from '... how long had *this* been going on? ...' to '... you scrawny wee mucker'.

1. Here is a list of key elements in this passage. Find a quotation to match each one.
   (a) Character interaction: Kirsty at odds with Chae's views (as ever!).
   (b) Characterisation: Chae's fiery sense of indignation.
   (c) Character/setting interaction: to demonstrate the closeness of the woods to Chae's heart.
   (d) Key event: a sentence which, in simple terms, sums up what has happened and points to the consequences.
   (e) Chae's anger builds to a climax.
2. Discuss how this passage is central to the theme of change.

Possible answers

1. (a) 'fine for Kinraddie the wood-men had been ... they'd paid high for their land'
   (b) '... how long had *this* been going on?'/'To hell with their board ... do you hear!'
   (c) 'he'd often minded of them out there in France, the woods, so bonny they were'
   (d) 'It would lay the whole Knapp open to the north-east now, and was fair the end of a living here'
   (e) 'And over at the office he had found ... you scrawny wee mucker' Conversation: tension builds to climax of Chae's furious question, 'And what sacrifices have you made ... mucker?'
2. Chae supports war and wants change for the better; shocked by a change for the worse (beauty/shelter of trees gone). Literal/metaphorical destruction of way of life: uncontrollable, unforeseen change can be instigated by war. The novel's warning to focus on humanity, not big solutions; change will destroy. Destruction of trees also foreshadows end of the novel: death of human beings.

Symbolism

Despite its basis in realism and characterisation, this is an extremely symbolic novel. People (and places) often represent ideas, emotionally charged events or social movements.

Spotlight on ... Chae as a symbol

Chae is used to signify the rise of an idealistic, disrespectful left-wing working class that believes the world can be improved by educating the poor to take on – and turn the tables on – their rich masters. He has spent time in Africa and identifies with the African people, not the imperialist Empire. However, he still remains patriotic – therefore he is an early volunteer for the British army.

When he sees the Kinraddie woods chopped down for the war effort, two symbols crash together. Chae has been optimistic that a fairer world will emerge from war's horrors. Thus the destruction of the sheltering, beautiful woods horrifies him. Is what he thought he was fighting for going to disappear? Chae favours progress within a sustainable, recognisable way of life (note also that the Tavendales seem to be achieving this before the intrusion of the war).

Discussion

Is Grassic Gibbon's final message about tradition and progress that they are incompatible?

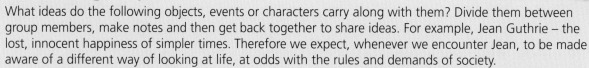

In small groups

What ideas do the following objects, events or characters carry along with them? Divide them between group members, make notes and then get back together to share ideas. For example, Jean Guthrie – the lost, innocent happiness of simpler times. Therefore we expect, whenever we encounter Jean, to be made aware of a different way of looking at life, at odds with the rules and demands of society.

- John Guthrie
- the standing stones
- Andy's rampage around Kinraddie
- the Reverend Gibbon
- Kinraddie itself
- Will
- the electric storm
- Chris herself

Possible answers

- Guthrie – the old Calvinist Scotland, a place of Protestant fundamentalism based around the work ethic and faith in a harsh God.
- The standing stones – the link with the past, the continuity of people on the land.
- Andy's rampage around Kinraddie – the suppressed sexuality of the Mearns. People love to gossip about it!
- The Reverend Gibbon – pseudo-respectable hypocrisy of religion as Grassic Gibbon saw it.
- Kinraddie itself – rural Scotland survived for many centuries and is now about to change.
- Will – a Scot abroad, seeking new opportunities and impatient with the past.
- The electric storm – foreshadows war, ironically, as the storm brings Ewan and Chris together. (Note the barbed wire – link with the Western Front.)
- Chris herself – Scotland: past, present and future. Also, the new twentieth-century woman: independent and able to choose her life.

Spotlight on ... Ewan

Intuitive and sensitive in his own way, a Highlander who is seen as being a bit different, with a certain innate elegance ('like a cat') and sexual magnetism, he is under-educated (compared with Chris) and can be influenced by war propaganda (compared with Rob). When he changes, we sense that he did not have the intellectual robustness to deal with the pressure, but realises he has blundered into 'betraying' Chris and all he truly believes in. Grassic Gibbon approves of his instinctive love of the land, but suggests that we need more than this to make our way in a complex world.

Climax

After the innocent contentment of Chris and Ewan's early life together, disruption comes in the form of war and the novel moves towards the tragic climax of their story. Character and thematic development are also important in this section, which begins when Ewan slips off to enlist in the army and ends with his ghostly or visualised 'return' to Chris.

On your own or with a partner

Examine the key moments for narrative, character and thematic elements. First there is the disappearance of Ewan. Read from 'And to Chris it seemed, then, Chae gone ...' to '... Ewan would be fine'.

1. What is the terrible contrast we see in these pages? As well as looking at what happens, think about Chris's feelings and the descriptions of Ewan.
2. How does the natural landscape help to underline Chris's changing emotions that evening?
3. Explain clearly why Ewan enlists.

Possible answers

1. Chris's plans for her new baby: full of love of life and the future versus Ewan's face 'dark and heavy' – he is distant, ill-tempered, then gone to face death, not create new life.

2. Many signs of spring life – animals, sounds, smells – all full of hope, but view of the destroyed wood and with no shelter from wind. Then the sounds of animals seeking shelter, emphasising the non-appearance of Ewan and the start of anxiety.

3. He could no longer cope with insults for 'cowardice', especially from fellow farmers.

With Ewan away, Chris's ability to cope becomes clear, either working with old Brigson, enjoying Will's visit (note the Will/Ewan contrast) or caring for Rob.

And then Ewan's visit: 'She had hardly been able to believe ... the whistle of his train out across the hills.' The description of their awful night together can be contrasted with their wedding night ('Seed-time': 'Then she forgot it ...') and after young Ewan's birth ('Harvest': 'But Chris didn't care ...').

In small groups

Ewan's visit can be seen as three main strands threaded together:

1. The change in Ewan: brutality and coarseness.
2. Chris: hurt, horrified and deeply puzzled.
3. Chris: defiant as her heart hardened, then her calm rejection of Ewan.

Each person in the group should take a strand and find two quotations that demonstrate it. Discuss what Grassic Gibbon is saying and how he is using language to do so. Here is one quotation for each strand to start you off:

1. 'a picture-book of young Ewan's lay there, he picked the thing up and flung it to the other side of the room'
2. 'But it wasn't Ewan, her Ewan, someone coarse and strange and strong had come back in his body to torment her'
3. 'And she smiled again, cold and secure and serene'

Note that there is also a change at the very end of the visit, reminiscent of her final response at John Guthrie's funeral.

Two major events regarding Ewan now happen:

- Chris is brought word of his death, and she reacts very badly to it.

- She is visited by Chae and learns the truth.

On your own or with a partner

1. The following quotations come from when Chris is brought word of Ewan's death. Explain the state of mind conveyed by each:
   (a) 'and she knew it was a lie'
   (b) 'and those bitches sat and spoke of their king and country'
   (c) 'but she'd finished with screaming, she went quiet and cold'
2. The visit of Chae ('Chae had lain in a camp nearby ... they killed him that morning').
   We can say that Chris's heart has died within her since hearing Ewan has died. By the end of Chae's account, she has come to terms with this. Consider Chae's words from Chris's point of view – as she sits there listening to Chae bravely telling her the difficult, potentially hugely upsetting truth. Note the irony that the very thing which, conventionally, Chris 'should' be ashamed of – Ewan's execution as a coward and deserter – is the thing that makes her most proud.
   (a) Which aspects of Chae's account are likely to have got through to Chris? Try to find two examples.
   (b) Explain why.

Possible answers

1. (a) Denial.
   (b) Fury and resentment.
   (c) Numbness of despair.
2. (a) Two possible examples:
       Chae tells her the truth immediately and directly.
       Chris cannot abide the platitudes with which people have tried to soften the impact of Ewan's death.
   (b) He tells her that Ewan 'minded Blawearie', and deserted. She begins to realise he died for what he loved.

The final reconciliation

Look again at the last short section of 'Harvest' (from 'Below them, Kinraddie' to the end.)

Scottish Text questions

Try these analysis questions based on this moment – the climax of Chris's character development, of her experience of loss, change, acceptance and keeping going – and, of course, for the love story of Chris and Ewan.

1. The opening paragraph conveys a sense of Chris's awareness of her past, present and (perhaps) future. By referring to both language and ideas, explain how this is achieved. **3**
2. The standing stones symbolise something very real and reassuring for Chris. By referring to the second paragraph, explain what this is and analyse how it is made clear. **3**
3. Look at paragraphs 3 and 4. Analyse how Grassic Gibbon uses language to create a powerful contrast in tone, from horrific to uplifting. **4**
4. Despite Ewan's shortcomings, Chris's love for him is authentic and convincing. By referring to this extract and elsewhere in the novel, discuss how Grassic Gibbon achieves this. **10**

Possible answers

1. The parallel structure of 'below ... above ... the loch ... young Ewan' contains the framework of her life at Blawearie – love of the land and her son/past and future.

   2 marks for a detailed/insightful comment plus a quotation/reference. 1 mark for a more basic comment plus a quotation/reference. 0 marks for a quotation with no comment. Total: 3 marks. (Marks can be gained 2+1 or 1+1+1. For full marks, both language and ideas must be covered.)

2. The standing stones represent stability, a place of comfort over the years. Removing her hand from the stone plunges her into uncertainty and unfulfilled longing.

   2 marks for a detailed/insightful comment plus a quotation/reference. 1 mark for a more basic comment plus a quotation/reference. 0 marks for a quotation with no comment. Total: 3 marks. (Marks can be gained 2+1 or 1+1+1. For full marks, both language and ideas must be covered.)

3. References to wounds and corpse-like ghost create a sense of the horror of Ewan's death. Then the focus on his eyes – the familiar 'light' of love for Chris in them suggests spiritual reconciliation.

   2 marks for a detailed/insightful comment plus a quotation/reference. 1 mark for a more basic comment plus a quotation/reference. 0 marks for a quotation with no comment. Total: 4 marks. (Marks can be gained 2+2, 2+1+1 or 1+1+1+1. For full marks, both sides of the contrast must be covered.)

4. **Up to 2 marks for a general explanation of Chris's love for Ewan in the novel (commonality). For example:**

   Grassic Gibbon's narrative style gives a strong sense of Chris's feelings, making us aware of the various things that bond them together such as passion and a shared love of the land.

   Up to 2 marks for comments on this section. For example:

   Contrast between the horror of war that has separated them – the bullet wound – and the 'light in his eyes that aye she could bring' – the sense of deep love lasting beyond death.

3 x 2 marks for comments and references from elsewhere in the novel, of which there are many. Here are some examples:

- The storm: working together in a dangerous, difficult situation creates a bonding experience, *or* romance and passion – kissing at the barn, the scent of honeysuckle as she is lost in wonder at the experience of passion.
- The wedding night: passion and feeling of 'rightness'; this is how life should be; total fulfilment.
- Together with young Ewan: more mature contentment as Chris lies in bed, between Ewan and young Ewan's cot; the richness of her joy and importance of physicality; 'body and blood and breath'. **Total: 10 marks.**

'Epilude'

Read from 'And it was only after he headed the leet ...' to '... The sleeked creature, who'd have thought it of her?'

Discussion

The war is over – and we have heard of the varying fortunes of the crofters, some of whom have indeed prospered among decay and loss. There is a new minister, the Reverend Colquhoun. What do you think of his role and his relationship with Chris?

Task

On your own

Think about the Epilude and the Prelude (both 'unfurrowed fields').

1. Why did Grassic Gibbon include the Prelude?
2. What picture does it provide of the Kinraddie of the novel?

Possible answers

1. It provides a framework, along with the Epilude, which is very useful in gauging the scale of the change which has come about. In itself, it gives an idea of the continuous change in views of the world and lifestyles which takes place even in a fairly settled rural community.

2. It shows us a Kinraddie that appears very settled, with its folk 'labelled' in their different roles – you will notice the prevalence of the derogatory community narrative voice (although Chae, Rob and Ewan come out of it fairly well) – and yet we are aware that they are at the temporary end of a long pathway of constant change.

The diagrams below trace Chris's development through the novel.

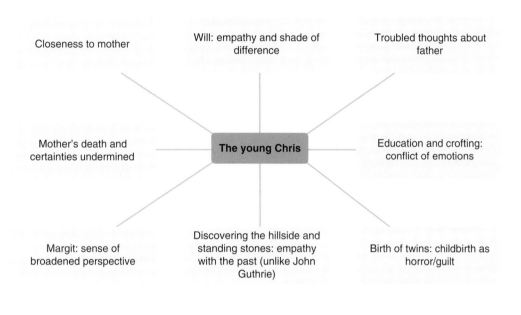

Closeness to mother

Will: empathy and shade of difference

Troubled thoughts about father

Mother's death and certainties undermined

The young Chris

Education and crofting: conflict of emotions

Margit: sense of broadened perspective

Discovering the hillside and standing stones: empathy with the past (unlike John Guthrie)

Birth of twins: childbirth as horror/guilt

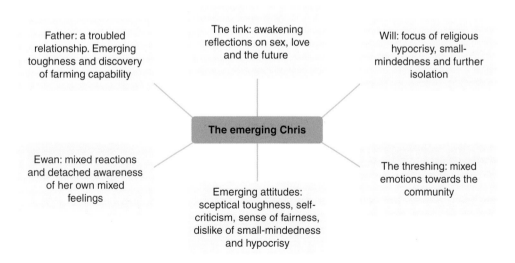

Father: a troubled relationship. Emerging toughness and discovery of farming capability

The tink: awakening reflections on sex, love and the future

Will: focus of religious hypocrisy, small-mindedness and further isolation

The emerging Chris

Ewan: mixed reactions and detached awareness of her own mixed feelings

Emerging attitudes: sceptical toughness, self-criticism, sense of fairness, dislike of small-mindedness and hypocrisy

The threshing: mixed emotions towards the community

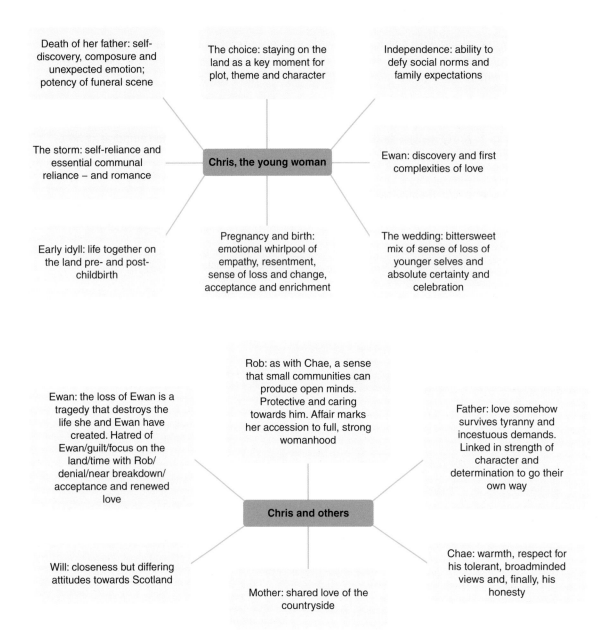

Death of her father: self-discovery, composure and unexpected emotion; potency of funeral scene

The choice: staying on the land as a key moment for plot, theme and character

Independence: ability to defy social norms and family expectations

The storm: self-reliance and essential communal reliance – and romance

Chris, the young woman

Ewan: discovery and first complexities of love

Early idyll: life together on the land pre- and post-childbirth

Pregnancy and birth: emotional whirlpool of empathy, resentment, sense of loss and change, acceptance and enrichment

The wedding: bittersweet mix of sense of loss of younger selves and absolute certainty and celebration

Rob: as with Chae, a sense that small communities can produce open minds. Protective and caring towards him. Affair marks her accession to full, strong womanhood

Ewan: the loss of Ewan is a tragedy that destroys the life she and Ewan have created. Hatred of Ewan/guilt/focus on the land/time with Rob/denial/near breakdown/acceptance and renewed love

Father: love somehow survives tyranny and incestuous demands. Linked in strength of character and determination to go their own way

Chris and others

Chae: warmth, respect for his tolerant, broadminded views and, finally, his honesty

Will: closeness but differing attitudes towards Scotland

Mother: shared love of the countryside

On your own or in small groups

As a final task, try to trace other characters through the novel, as the diagrams above do with Chris. Look at:

- John Guthrie: what are the positives and negatives in his character? Think of his relationships with Jean, Will, Chris, his neighbours, his God, those who think they are his superiors.
- Will: compare his attitudes to Scotland and Argentina – what creates his contempt and bitterness?
- Chae: we have looked at his symbolic qualities, but do not forget the interesting human traits of his character which Grassic Gibbon obviously enjoyed creating – his naivety, optimism and drive.
- Rob: sceptical, independent of mind – he is there to be admired. What does he add to the novel?
- Ewan: he has the earth in his blood, and is Chris's soulmate, but what are his limitations?

PROSE SHORT STORIES
BY GEORGE MACKAY BROWN

George Mackay Brown lived most of his life in Orkney, apart from brief spells studying and working on the Scottish mainland. This brilliant man had a troubled life, plagued by poverty and ill health. After training as a teacher in Edinburgh, he returned to Orkney in 1961 and his collection of stories, *A Time to Keep*, was published in 1969. Not surprisingly, this was immediately successful, and he went on to write a wealth of brilliant poetry and longer prose as well as short stories and works for children. Despite his success, Mackay Brown was never comfortable with fame. His religious faith was very important to him in terms of making sense of the world.

The world of Mackay Brown's stories blends together elements of Viking and Scottish culture, Christian and Pagan religion to create a picture which is uniquely Orcadian. In his work, he examined the permanence of nature and the farming/fishing life: he was critical of 'progress', which he regarded as spiritually empty. Many of these ideas are reflected in the six stories you will be studying for your Scottish Text section. These are:

- 'A Time to Keep'
- 'The Whaler's Return'
- 'The Wireless Set'
- 'The Bright Spade'
- 'Tartan'
- 'The Eye of the Hurricane'.

The stories are set in Orkney or the isolated, northern Scottish coast and deal with the following themes:

- harsh, uncompromising nature (both on land and at sea)
- the influence of the small, close-knit community on the individual
- the complicated relationship between island life and the external world
- tradition and progress
- life and death
- flawed humanity struggling to find meaning and fulfilment.

The setting of the remote island community is not just a background but an integral part of the development of character and theme.

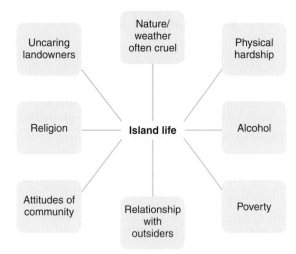

The stories are set during different time periods. Some, such as 'A Time to Keep' and 'The Whaler's Return', do not have a definite time period: they deal with a traditional way of life – the sea and the crofting – which was disappearing by the mid-twentieth century. Others are more certain: 'The Wireless Set' is told during the Second World War, and 'Tartan' during the time of the Vikings. However, the key themes of the stories are timeless.

You may have read through all the stories already; alternatively, you might be working through them one by one. This book can be used for either approach.

Story 1: 'A Time to Keep'

This story describes a year in the life of Bill, a fisherman/crofter, who narrates the story. It is a journey from winter to winter and, in this year, he experiences marriage, birth, death and a kind of 'rebirth'.

The opening

Let's start by examining the opening of 'A Time to Keep'. Read from 'We came down through the fields' to 'The first true fire had been lit'. Mackay Brown's style is stark and pared down to the essentials, which means the reader can enjoy teasing out the meaning.

The wedding

In the opening sentence, 'We came down through the fields, Ingi and I', intimacy is established through the use of pronouns ('We ... I') and Ingi's name: they are together on their journey. Having left their own wedding, they walk the ten miles (over the hills, with snow falling) to their croft. What is suggested by these simple statements?

- Traditional for bride and groom to leave before the wedding dance ends, but also note that the community carries on celebrating regardless of the involvement of any specific people. The community lives on and no one within it is indispensable.

- The journey home: 'Ten miles ... lacings of snow ... upper hills were white.' No mention of the physical hardship of the walk; accepted as a necessary part of life, with 'lacings' of snow providing a frisson of excitement.

- On arrival, no hugging or carrying over the threshold: it is straight to work: Ingi in the house, Bill in the byre. A practical and hardworking life, where male and female roles are clearly defined.

Their home

- '... a clean new house of sea-washed stones ... no earth-weathering on the walls yet.' This conveys hope, a sense of a new start, with the ever-present elemental force of the sea, currently benign – cleansing the stones of their house. The house not eroded by storms or damp – 'yet'. With the walls, 'springy heather' and stones on the roof, their home has 'emerged' from the land: their lives will be intrinsically bound up in nature.

- Bill built the house himself; the mason built the byre, barn and stable. Are these farm buildings more important, so the professionals are called in? Or does the tradition of self-sufficiency and male pride mean that the home he builds is most important?

- Fires are lit to counteract the damp – functional, rather than for comfort. A building, not yet a home.

- The croft is adequately, yet modestly, equipped with precise numbers of livestock: 'two cows' and 'seven sheep'. New plough, 'a grey powerful curve', suggesting strength and potential farming success. A new beginning.

What is missing from this opening?

There is no reference to love, although they are newly married and arriving home together. However, do not think this is because the feelings themselves are missing. 'This was our croft, Ingi's and mine ... Blue smoke was rising ... The first true fire had been lit.' There is a beautifully understated closeness in these words.

So, we have intimacy, hope, the promise of a new life together, a fresh beginning, a community that is there in the background ... that's a lot from an apparently very simple description of events. As you read the stories, you will become accustomed to Mackay Brown's subtle and effective style.

Task

With a partner

Read section 2 of the story (from 'I was in ...' to '... before me'). Things start to go wrong for Bill and Ingi. What aspects of character, plot, setting and theme development can you spot? What do you notice about the following?

- Closeness between Bill and Ingi.
- Bill's self-sufficiency and pride.
- The role of the community.
- Any other warning signs.

Possible answers

- **Closeness between Bill and Ingi:** there are three direct references to Ingi: 'I left Ingi in our bed' (describing his usual mornings); 'I didn't feel the need of anyone except Ingi' (explaining why he didn't bother to communicate much with the other fishermen); 'And always when I reached the door Ingi stood there before me' (in the evenings). These all suggest a close, intimate relationship, so close in fact that other friendships seem unnecessary. Reference to the fire: 'the flame beat in the hearth and the house was alive'. Fire is associated with home, warmth (metaphorical as well as literal) and love throughout the story.
- **Bill's self-sufficiency and pride:** we are told that Bill made his boat with his 'own hands' and carries the haddocks home after fishing. He is, so far, supporting Ingi and himself.

→

- **The role of the community:** we see that, for some reason, Bill is not accepted: the other fishermen 'kept apart from me. I was like a stranger in the valley.' No explanation is given for this but it seems to be, at least partly, linked to his marriage, as they were friendly before. What is also interesting is Bill's reaction: he tries neither to make friends nor find out the reason for their coldness: 'I was, it seemed, unpopular', he says, apparently accepting this state of affairs. He does not need them or care about their opinions.
- **Any other warning signs:** Bill's nonchalance towards the community's opinions is in itself a sign of potential trouble: the community is not just a background to people's lives in the islands but an integral part of their way of life. Bill and Ingi, isolated from the people around them, will struggle to cope in the hard life ahead of them. There is also, perhaps, another hint: when Bill goes down to the shore in the morning, he is always last there. Is this because he is avoiding the others, or vice versa? Or is he already showing a lack of commitment to his role as provider? Also note that the fire's smoke is now 'sometimes blue, sometimes black'. The black smoke, shadowy and mysterious, is ominous.

Now read the rest of the story, if you have not already done so.

Narrative structure

The plot of 'A Time to Keep', like that of all six Mackay Brown stories on the list, is simple. It has a 'classic' narrative structure, following this pattern:

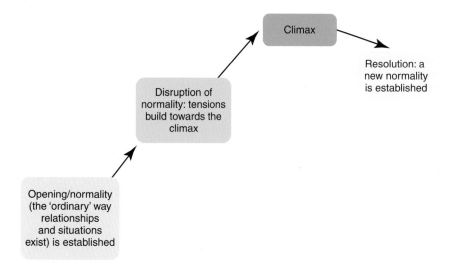

Remember that disruption can be caused by one decisive event or it can be signalled by a series of smaller events that build up the tension. Resolution does not necessarily mean a 'happy' ending: it just means that whatever tension has been built up is now resolved. This can be a tragic ending or acceptance of a new, less happy, way of life.

With a partner

Try plotting the events of 'A Time to Keep' following the narrative structure in the diagram above.

- Opening: Bill and Ingi set up home.
- Disruption/building tension: Bill works at fishing and less successfully at crofting. Tensions rise: he drinks, Ingi is lonely, he refuses to go to church. Her father attempts to help and interfere.
- Climax: Ingi dies in childbirth.
- Resolution: Bill pledges himself to his son and finds a way to carry on.

A narrative structure exercise like this is a good starting point for any prose text you are studying. Try it with the other Mackay Brown stories on the list.

Characters

Bill is at the centre of the story, both as main character and as narrator. Let's examine him in more detail.

With a partner

There are a number of forces acting on Bill: both internal (within him) and external (which he cannot necessarily control). Make a list of at least four of each of these and then discuss how important each one is.

For example, Bill's determination to reject religion is mentioned a number of times and is a cause of tension, not just between him and the general community but between him and Ingi, who truly believes and wants Bill to go to church with her.

Internal forces	External forces

Get together with another pair to discuss your choices. Do not worry if you disagree with others about which forces are more important: different people may have different, equally valid, views. The important thing is to be able to justify your opinions.

Internal forces	External forces
His own moods	Nature/weather – crops destroyed
Weakness, e.g. alcohol	Community pressure to conform, e.g. religion
Stubbornness	Ingi's father's desire to control them
Love for Ingi	Unsympathetic landowner
Desire for independence	Sea-storm destroyed his lobster pots
Desire to provide for his family	Suspicion of other crofters/fishermen

Bill's conflict with others

With a partner

Find quotations to match each of the following statements about Bill's key areas of conflict with those around him.

1. Bill clashes with the landowner's factor about his newly ploughed land.
2. He does not go to church because he thinks religion is nonsense.
3. He is accused by his neighbours of stealing lobster pots and reacts angrily.
4. He is angry when Ingi's father attempts to lecture him.
5. He refuses to help at the Two-Waters' harvest.
6. He refuses to accept conditions to the loan of money Ingi's father gives him.
7. The women send him away during Ingi's childbirth, blaming him for her suffering.
8. He is revolted by the trite religious comments made by the missionary and others.
9. He is, at first, very unpleasant to Anna of Two-Waters.

Possible answers

1. 'Did you never hear of the Crofters' Act of 1888?'

2. 'All the women ... listening to that fairy tale.'

3. 'I'm not a thief ... but you're a liar.'

4. 'Ingi and I, we don't want your money.'

5. 'Keep your mouth shut ... and maybe you'll get more harvesters.'

6. 'I was not buying two hundred and fifty pounds worth of hypocrisy.'

7. 'You clear off ... harshly at me.'

8. ' – most of them lies – ... a welter of sentimental mush.'

9. '"Get away out of here, you ugly bitch," I shouted at her.'

Bill's relationship with Ingi

This is the central relationship in the story. The story is, really, their story – from their wedding day until Ingi's death, almost a year later – and Bill's reaction to this tragedy.

With a partner

Now for a more detailed look at Ingi's relationship with Bill. Read the quotations below and decide, in each case, what we are really being told about the relationship between them.

1. 'We leaned towards each other then and kissed in the darkness.'
2. '"You'll be fine now ... Your throat must be dry. I'll get you some water."'
3. 'I had more kindness than usual from Ingi when I got back from that interview.'
4. 'We came home stung with clegs, blistered by the sun, and too sore to eat or make love.'
5. 'One morning Ingi was very sick.'
6. '"Yes, come inside, please," said Ingi.'
7. '"Ingi," I said, "here's what you're going to get, a pair of new black shoes and a coat and a hat for the kirk on Sabbath."'
8. '... I saw the beach and a solitary woman standing on it ... Ingi, a figure still as stone.'
9. '"We must repay hatred with kindness," she said. "Anna was very hurt."'
10. 'Inside, Ingi cried out. I turned away in a panic.'
11. 'Ingi lay in the bed, long and pale as a quenched candle.'

Possible answers

Quotations 1 and 4 suggest their physical intimacy, as does the hint of pregnancy in quotation 5, leading to childbirth, when Bill desperately fears losing her (quotation 10).

Quotations 2 and 8 show Ingi's devotion to Bill, although quotation 3 suggests things were not always harmonious. Ingi's shame at Bill's refusal to consider the community's view is shown in quotations 6 and 9. Quotation 7 shows Bill's determination to provide for her (and spite her father).

Finally, quotation 11 is a simple statement of absolute grief, as she lies, beautiful and lifeless, before him.

Themes and style

One key theme of this story is the unending struggle of flawed humanity to gain fulfilment, the fight against the hard things in life. Now that you know the story well, you will understand how Mackay Brown uses narrative, plot and setting to develop this theme. Bill, the main character, is far from perfect, but he does have his genuinely imaginative and almost heroic moments. Through his struggle with the hardships of life, Mackay Brown says something about human beings in general.

One memorable feature of style is the use of first-person narrative. Remember that, as a character with a specific perspective, Bill is an unreliable narrator. We cannot just accept his view on everything as being 'correct' or the only valid viewpoint. Bear that in mind when tackling the following tasks.

Task

On your own or with a partner

Answer these questions linking theme to other aspects of the story.

1. 'A green offering hand, our valley, corn-giver, fire-giver, water-giver, keeper of men and beasts. The other hand that fed us was this blue hand of the sea, which was treacherous, which had claws to it, which took more than ever it gave.' These are Bill's thoughts. How do these words develop character and theme?

2. 'The black keening I could have endured.' After Ingi's death, why could Bill have 'endured' the long, wailing lamentation of women in traditional mourning but could not stand the Christian comments of consolation?

3. 'Be honest ... Be against all darkness. Fight on the side of life. Be against ministers, lairds, shopkeepers. Be brave always.' Explain these words of 'blessing' that Bill says to his son.

4. 'There were times I could scarcely look into the shifting pool of his face; the skull stared back at me through a thousand trembling resemblances.' Why does Bill react like this to his son's face?

5. 'Anna broke the red core with the poker; flames flowered everywhere in the fireplace, and the room was suddenly alive with the rosy shifting dapple.' Why is it significant that Anna now tends the fire in the house?

Possible answers

1. Bill is clearly an imaginative character who intuitively understands that the sea, though a provider, is also a killer. It is impersonal; it does not care. This ties in with the theme of the harshness of island life.

2. Bill would have found the pagan wailing sincere and meaningful but scorns the Christian consolation as empty hypocrisy.

3. Bill wants his son to embody the qualities he admires and sees so rarely: qualities he has striven, but often failed, to achieve.

4. Bill can hardly bear the pain of seeing the resemblance between his son and the dead Ingi.

5. Anna has 'replaced' Ingi as home-maker, surrogate mother and – it is hinted – new partner of Bill. Their relationship is far from the passionate intensity of Bill and Ingi's love: more practical and, perhaps, more likely to survive in a harsh world. Look back at the start of the story and compare it to the ending (from 'Anna came through the fields ...').

Story 2: 'The Whaler's Return'

The story is simple: Andrew Flaws, who has returned from an Arctic summer of whaling, makes his way from the port of Hamnavoe to his home in Birsay. This is quite a long trek and there are many difficulties on the way. His arduous walk home is also an allegory for the journey of people through life, facing challenges along the way.

Flaws has already faced death on the whaling ship – both from nature and, even more dangerous, humanity – and now he should be safe, but the road home is full of temptations. His main problem is keeping out of the various pubs along the way. Flaws wants to get home with his money more or less intact but, as his name suggests, he is only human and, like Bill in 'A Time to Keep', makes mistakes.

Narrative structure

Let's start by examining the events of Flaws's walk itself. This provides the simple structure of the narrative, building to the climax, when he faces the biggest danger, and then reaches Peterina's house, tired and poorer than when he set out – but safe.

There are six stages before he reaches Peterina's house, his final destination. At each he is urged to drink and parts with some of his precious money (needed for his new life). At each stage, he is encouraged by someone to do something: usually this is a temptation to act against his better judgement, although occasionally he does something good.

Task

With a partner

Plan the events of the story, identifying the opening, disruption/building tension, climax and resolution. Use this diagram to help you:

```
            Climax
           /      \
          /        \
     Disruption   Resolution
        /
       /
   Opening
```

You will have noticed that most of the places he stops in are pubs ('The Arctic Whaler', 'The White Horse', 'Halvo's Ale House') or festivities (the tinkers' wedding). He is tempted by the conviviality, the life of immediate gratification rather than saving thriftily for the future. He is also tempted by beautiful women and at one point pretends to be something he is not, in order to impress. At the houses of Bella Jean Bews and the minister, he settles the shrouding and burial debts of Peterina's father. These are good deeds – though, again, he enjoys a drink while doing them.

Flaws's story ends happily – or, at least, moderately happily. He arrives home safely, with some money left, ready to begin a new life.

Characters

There is only one developed character, Flaws himself. Everyone else he meets along the way – even Peterina waiting back home – represents challenges, goals and temptations that he endeavours to deal with.

Task

On your own or with a partner

From your knowledge of the narrative, note down your first impressions of Flaws. Get together with another pair to share your ideas.

Discussion

Andrew Flaws is clearly not a particularly heroic man. However, his 'sins' are not active or aggressive: he does not go out of his way to look for trouble. Rather, he allows things to happen to him. He encounters situations and reacts to them. When he does 'wrong', he does feel ashamed, but this does not stop him from behaving irresponsibly the next time temptation comes around. He is, in short, a flawed and troubled human being – trying to do his best, but aware that he will stumble and fall, again and again.

Task

On your own or with a partner

One thing the final Scottish text question asks you to do is to make comparisons. So, let's begin by comparing the main characters in the two stories we have read so far.

Which of the men does the following?	Bill	Flaws
Holds a grudge		
Wants to be accepted by others		
Feels protected by religious faith		
Thinks independently		
Attempts to do the right thing		
Feels responsible for others		
Sincerely loves the woman in his life		
Treats his family (in law) with traditional respect		
Is weak when it comes to alcohol		

Task

With a partner

As in 'A Time to Keep', the key relationship in 'The Whaler's Return' is between the main character and the woman he loves, with her father there in the background. There are interesting similarities and differences between the trios in these two stories. Discuss any similarities and/or differences between the two trios. Remember that, in the final Scottish text question, you will need to make comparisons.

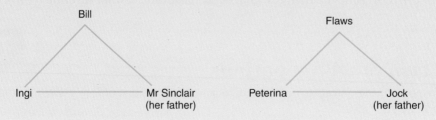

Discussion

While Bill and Ingi love each other deeply, Flaws and Peterina seem to have a much more practical, less romantic arrangement. Flaws finds other women attractive and there is the comment that Peterina is 'rather ugly'. Yet she represents stability and security: a future with her is the driving force behind Flaws's journey and he is relieved to reach the safety of her house. She has the down-to-earth approach and skills needed for the hard island life (unlike the more delicate Ingi). In both relationships, the woman's father is important. Mr Sinclair (Ingi's father) is caring and concerned – to the point of interfering. Peterina's father, Jock, is a hard man, not missed by anyone, including Peterina, after his death. His death, and the expense of the funeral, causes Peterina to live in shame and give Flaws the chance to do 'a good thing' by paying her debts.

Setting/theme

One theme of the story is the struggle to do the right thing in a world full of temptations. Let's look at how the climax and resolution of the story develop this theme.

Climax

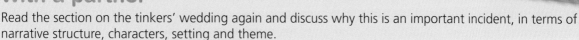

Task

With a partner

Read the section on the tinkers' wedding again and discuss why this is an important incident, in terms of narrative structure, characters, setting and theme.

Possible answers

1. **Narrative structure:** this, the climax of the story, is where Flaws faces his greatest temptations (the tinker girl, the fiery spirits she gives him and the excitement of the tinker camp) and the greatest dangers ('lured' in by the girl, he is attacked by her comrades in a savage moment: 'Then the black snarling wave was all about him.')

2. **Characters:** we see Flaws tempted by the wild excitement of the tinkers' way of life, which is so different from the hard life of toil ahead of him. The wedding ceremony has a compelling drama about it: an elemental quality. The tinker girl appears in only this one incident, but her character is effectively drawn in subtle hints, for example '... she was off like a shadow'. Flaws 'wanted to kiss her before he gave his kisses to Peterina for ever.' In a twist, it is she who reports him to the tinker men, who attack him.

3. **Setting/theme:** the tinkers appear to live outside convention and therefore they represent the kind of temptation that attracts Flaws. Yet they have strict rules of their own and defend their privacy fiercely (hence the attack on Flaws). The ceremony that attracts him by its wildness is a wedding, which mirrors while also providing a contrast with the wedding Flaws is heading home for. The tinker wedding is primitive – almost primeval – with the mixing of urine and screeching of accusations. Husband and wife accepting each other, flaws and all, provides a parallel for the practical, accepting relationship of Flaws and Peterina.

Resolution

With a partner

Now try the same type of analysis on the story's ending. Make notes on the following topics and find quotations to support your ideas.

- Narrative structure: how does the end of the story 'resolve' Flaws's story?
- Characters: what do we learn about Flaws, Peterina and their relationship in this section?
- Setting: explain how the community is important in this section.
- Theme: which themes does this section develop?

Possible answers

- **Narrative structure:** Peterina's home is the final destination, the safe haven at the end of Flaws's journey. There is an atmosphere of peace and calm after the dangers and temptations he has faced.
- **Characters:**
  - Flaws's sense of responsibility is clear: 'I saw to all that' and 'Everything is paid' – simple, sweeping statements that he has provided for her; he has immediate plans for work and will fish that afternoon (despite exhaustion); he has practical ideas for the future (harvesters required) and settles down to his new life immediately; 'I have the rent for the croft of Breck' – he has still managed to keep this vital money back – he is certain of the next step; 'You're in better shape ...' – Peterina acknowledges his (relatively) responsible behaviour on the way home.
  - Peterina is sensible, matter-of-fact, not over-emotional, caring (in an understated way); she describes her father's death simply and gives his name 'formally'; she will make the blanket, christening shawl and shrouds – marriage, birth and death are contemplated in a practical way.
- **Setting:** Peterina has relied on community charity to pay the necessary fees relating to her father's death (positive community role), but she is ashamed to be seen in public as a result, which suggests community criticism, although clearly it is not her fault.
- **Theme:** flawed humanity struggles to cope in a harsh world; death is part of life.

Story 3: 'The Wireless Set'

'The Wireless Set' is a beautifully crafted piece. Having studied the previous two stories, what can we expect from this one?

- A simple structure involving an opening, disruption, building up to a climax and resolution.

- Characters who 'get on with life' despite their problems and life of hardship.

- Deeply felt but unexpressed emotion.

- The importance of the community and the outside world.

> 'The Wireless Set' is set during the Second World War: a significant intrusion from the outside world into island life. The war is far removed from the islanders, yet it takes away their sons. It intrudes in the form of reports via the wireless set (radio).
>
> Remember that this story takes place in the days when there was no television and a radio was a pretty hi-tech piece of equipment, especially in a remote, rural location like Tronvik. So it represents progress, the modern world, which comes into conflict with the traditional life led by the folk of the valley.

On your own

To prepare for your work on this story, carry out some background research on the internet by searching for 'Lord Haw-Haw (William Joyce)'. Find out about his role in pro-Nazi propaganda.

On your own

Begin with a quick narrative structure exercise. List the main events, decide how they relate to each other (the sequence or cause–effect relationship) and how they fit into the pattern of opening – disruption/ building tension – climax – resolution.

Element of narrative structure	Main events and how they relate to each other
Opening – establishing normality	
Disruption – events building to the climax	
Climax	
Resolution – this could be very close to the climax	

Characters

In this story, we have a character trio of Howie – who bought the wireless set – and his parents, Old Hugh and Betsy. Their family relationship – and the wireless set's intrusion into their life – forms the basis of the story. Let's begin by looking at the opening of the story and the establishment of Howie's personality.

In groups of three

Read the following quotations, which are about – or said by – Howie when he returns home from a season at the whaling (like Flaws in 'The Whaler's Return'). Work out what Mackay Brown is suggesting about Howie, his attitude to the outside world and his role in introducing the wireless set to his parents. Take three quotations each. Make notes on each of your quotations, and then get back together to compare ideas.

1. 'he arrived ... with a stuffed wallet and jingling pockets'
2. 'he brought presents for everyone in Tronvik'
3. 'Everyone ... crowded into the but-end of the croft, as Howie unwrapped and distributed his gifts'
4. '"Have you prayed every night, and not sworn?"
   "This is thine, mother," said Howie.'
5. '"It's a wireless set," said Howie proudly.'
6. '"Everybody in the big cities has a wireless," said Howie.'
7. 'But now Tronvik has a wireless set as well, and maybe we're not such clodhoppers as they think.'
8. '"This wireless speaks the truth," said Howie.'
9. 'In September that same year war broke out, and Howie and three other lads from the valley joined the minesweepers.'

Possible answers

Quotations 1, 2 and 3 suggest Howie's generosity and eagerness to spend his money on others – on everyone, in fact. Is there a hint of naive self-importance in his desire to show off by bringing presents for everyone?

Quotation 4 is interesting because of what is *not* said, as well as what *is* said. When his mother asks if he is being a 'good boy', he avoids the question but talks about the wireless set instead.

Quotations 5, 6 and 7 show Howie's pride in what he has introduced to the valley: a touch of sophistication, culture and 'civilisation'. Clearly he feels that the valley was lacking these qualities before: when he says 'they' think the valley people are 'clodhoppers', it is not just 'they' who think this.

Quotations 8 and 9 show Howie's faith in the outside world to provide enlightenment as well as excitement and opportunity. His naivety is indicated in his commitment to the wireless set as a source of 'truth'. (If he really were sophisticated, he would realise it is a source of propaganda. Even the simple valley folk can tell that the weather forecasts are inaccurate, while the advertisements are dismissed as 'a kind of loud half-witted voice'.) The fact that he volunteers to join the minesweepers (a particularly dangerous job) as soon as the war begins shows his enthusiasm for the 'doing his bit'. He has, clearly, believed the government's message that the war will be won easily, that the soldiers are heroes and that it will be a glorious adventure. This acceptance of its message leads to his death.

In small groups

You will notice that, after joining up, Howie never features in the story until the news of his death. Focus now on Old Hugh, Betsy and the missionary (minister). Try to find three key quotations and, as in the exercise above, explain why each one is important. Then get together to compare notes. Try to spot contrasts and similarities, links to theme and any effective uses of language.

Themes

In this story we can see how Mackay Brown blends narrative, characters and the wartime island setting together skilfully to develop the themes: the dangers of naive trust in the 'outsiders' or 'authorities', and the destructive nature of war itself.

The voice of William Joyce, 'Lord Haw-Haw' (the most prominent broadcaster on the 'Germany Calling' Nazi radio station), comes to represent the deceitful wiles of the outside world. The islanders' view of him is that he embodies 'a kind of bestial joviality ... that at once repelled and fascinated them'. Note that their feelings of repugnance (and attraction) have nothing to do with patriotism or anti-German feeling: it is more a sense of horrified amazement in his skill as an outrageous liar.

The wireless set, of course, does not actually cause the death of Howie or any of the other men killed in the war. The set represents the outside world, the world of lies and propaganda. When Hugh smashes it up, he is trying clumsily to erase the cause of all the suffering – to get rid of the war itself and to kill the enemy that has so cruelly taken his son from him.

On your own or with a partner

Read the following list of examples of lies 'told' by the wireless set. In each case, explain why each is significant in building up towards the climax, the news of Howie's death. The first one has been done for you.

Example	Significance
The night the wireless arrives: forecast of rain affecting fishing	The days are fair – Hugh and Howie 'harvest' the lobsters. This shows that Hugh's specific rural know-how has more relevance than the generalised forecast from mainland Britain
That winter: France will not fall to the Germans	
The aircraft carrier *Ark Royal* has been sunk in the Mediterranean	
The people of Britain are starving	

The final example, the message about 'starving Britain' that they listen to while feasting on 'bloody pudding' (black pudding), buttered bannocks and ale, is a particularly ironic example of the lies told by the wireless. The image of Betsy, a bit tipsy on her own ale – thrusting 'the hissing frying pan under the nose – so to speak – of the wireless' to prove it is wrong – is a richly comical one. The shock of Howie's death, in the very next episode of the story, is all the greater.

In small groups

The story reaches a climax with the news of Howie's death and the reaction of his parents. Discuss:

- what happens
- how Mackay Brown makes this part effective.

Story 4: 'The Bright Spade'

In this story, the theme of humanity versus the hardships of an uncompromising, tough life is presented in a particularly extreme way. The story is just over three pages long (the shortest story of the six) and the opening sentence sets the tone: 'That winter the gravedigger was the busiest man in the island.'

The narrative is extremely simple: it charts the deaths of various people over the course of one particularly harsh winter. The setting is vital: the fragility of such a remote island community, dependent on the elements, is emphasised in this catalogue of deaths, mostly due directly or indirectly to the way of life they endure. The setting in time is left indeterminate, but it is presumably before the 'luxuries' of shops selling food throughout the winter and emergency services available to help a community in crisis. Characterisation, too, is reduced to the minimum: the only developed character is Jacob the gravedigger – and even he is little more than a series of reactions and attitudes – while the other characters are pared down to a basic description of their deaths and an indication of how Jacob was paid for digging their graves.

However, do not be deceived into thinking this is a simple or insignificant story. It is a very skilful piece of writing, full of lyrical power and effective thematic development. It can also be seen as an allegory for human suffering and struggle, and some of its elements seem closer to myth than realism. Its very simplicity allows us to see how narrative, character, setting and style are entwined to develop the chilling theme.

Read the story's second sentence: 'They got the thin harvest in and then the wind squatted in the east, a winter witch, and blew the island grey with her breath.' What does Mackay Brown achieve in this relatively short sentence? We have a strong sense of nature as a malignant force: the devastating wind 'a winter witch', squatting like some monster, blowing death all over the island, which becomes 'grey' – colourless and lifeless as a result. All from one sentence!

Task

On your own, with a partner or in small groups

Make a list of the various deaths which take place over that harsh winter. Think about what Mackay Brown is telling us about this community through the list of deaths.

1. How many of the deaths are linked (directly or indirectly) to the harshness of nature?
2. What do you notice about the pace of deaths, starting in October, as the winter progresses?
3. Why does the laird's son need a deep grave, whereas the fiddler of Cornquoy needs a narrow grave?
4. Why do you think that the ages of Abraham (94) and the girl from the Glebe (16) are mentioned?
5. Do you think there is a significance in the number of sailors and valley men killed by the elements?
6. How many people pay Jacob with money? How many do not pay him at all?
7. What does the sequence of events emphasise about death in this island community?
8. Mackay Brown's style is spare and stark, yet there are examples of beautiful images from nature in amongst the sense of nature as a harsh force. Try to find three examples of these.

Possible answers

1. Virtually all of them (with one or possibly two exceptions).

2. The sense of pace quickens: the scale is escalating.

3. The laird's son is rich whereas the fiddler is poor, so this is a reflection on the girth of the people/ the size of the bodies.

4. It shows that all ages fall victim.

5. The number seven has magical or mythological significance in stories. The seven outsiders who die are matched by the islanders who sacrifice themselves in an attempt to save the community.

6. Only one (the laird) pays in money; two pay nothing; the rest pay with 'whatever they can'.

7. That death is ever-present in the community.

8. 'clung to life like the last tattered leaf on a branch'; 'the fiddle, once a sweet brimming shell, hung at Jacob's wall like a shrivelled chrysalis'; 'like a troop of spectres'.

Task

On your own

1. Jacob is more of a symbolic figure than a fully rounded character (compare with Bill and Flaws). What do you think Jacob represents?
2. His 'bright spade' could be seen as another version of which other (originally agricultural) implement?
3. Jacob does, however, have a discernible personality. What evidence is there that he:
   (a) can be weak and self-indulgent?
   (b) can be selfish and demanding?
   (c) nonetheless has a basic decency?

Possible answers

1. Jacob is a figure of death.

2. His spade could be seen to substitute a scythe.

3. (a) He drank all the whisky.
   (b) He demanded payment for burying the sailors.
   (c) He took no payment for the seven islanders.

Scottish Text questions

Read from 'One night there was ...' to 'in the island', then tackle these analysis questions.

1.	Explain the impact of the story of the old man of Cornquoy's death.	**2**
2.	Analyse how Mackay Brown uses language to describe the old man's fiddle.	**4**
3.	Analyse how Mackay Brown's use of language effectively describes the events following the men's decision to seek food.	**4**
4.	In his short stories, Mackay Brown deals with the relationship between life and death. By referring to this and at least one other story, discuss how he does this.	**10**

Possible answers

1. Horror of dog eating leg/even this is described in a matter-of-fact way, as if it is a commonplace event/community involvement – break down door to find him (though he has been dead for a while).

   Any two for 1 mark each (1+1). Total: 2 marks.

2. 'sweet brimming shell' suggests full of music; 'liquid' tones – emphasis on life and beauty; contrast with image of death 'like a shrivelled chrysalis' – life has gone out of it, empty; fiddle has 'died' – metaphor for the beauty he brings through his music.

   2 marks for a detailed/insightful comment plus a quotation/reference. 1 mark for a more basic comment plus a quotation/reference. 0 marks for a quotation with no comment. Total: 4 marks. (Marks can be gained 2+2, 2+1+1 or 1+1+1+1.)

3. 'worst blizzard of the winter descended' – intensity of storm; 'great swirling blankets of snow' – overwhelming, covering everything; 'like a troop of spectres' – foreshadowing deaths; 'Tinkers saw' – they have passed into folklore.

   2 marks for a detailed/insightful comment plus a quotation/reference. 1 mark for a more basic comment plus a quotation/reference. 0 marks for a quotation with no comment. Total: 4 marks. (Marks can be gained 2+2, 2+1+1 or 1+1+1+1.)

4. **Up to 2 marks for a general explanation of how the harshness of the environment is dealt with in the stories (commonality). For example:**

   Life and death are very close/death is ever present; harshness of the environment.

   Up to 2 marks for comments on this section. For example:

   Even the strongest men cannot survive the elements; a man who created such beautiful music is now reduced to a macabre vision of a dog and a leg.

→

3 x 2 marks for comments and references from other short stories, of which there are many. Here are some examples:

- 'A Time to Keep': Ingi, with her whole life ahead of her, dies while (ironically) giving new life.
- 'A Time to Keep': fear of drowning/storms when fishing – a part of Bill's daily life/Ingi waiting anxiously on the shore.
- 'The Whaler's Return': making shrouds is a preparation for a wedding – death always anticipated.

Total: 10 marks.

Story 5: 'Tartan'

This story again explores the relationship between community and outsiders: in this case, Viking raiders. It is unusual in the selection in that it is told from the point of view of the outsiders, and the story does not exactly conform to the conventional idea of marauding Vikings and terrified victims. True, the Vikings have come on a raid looking for anything they can take back with them, but they must be among the least successful Viking raiders in history! If anything, the Durness (northern mainland Scotland) community is the brooding presence, building in strength as the story develops. The only human casualty is Kol, a Viking whose throat is cut as he lies drunk outside one of the cottages. The only money that changes hands is the silver Byzantine coin given to the boy by the Vikings. As for seizing the women of the island? Arnor says he would like to cure the dark-haired woman's 'loneliness' but, by the time he looks up at her, she is 'three fields' away. He is never a serious threat. The sum of the Vikings' 'plunder' is two sheep (which they struggle to get on board), a pot of soup, some ale and a bale of tartan cloth.

Mackay Brown is not casting the Vikings as 'villains': their history is, after all, closely involved with that of Scotland. (Vikings travelled from Scandinavia and settled in various parts of Britain, including Orkney and the northern coast of Scotland; they were not just the violent rampagers of stories.) Instead, he develops the Vikings' trek across the island as an allegory, commenting on aspects of humanity.

In small groups

The Vikings 'visit' five homes:

- empty house where they see the sheep
- empty house – except for a pot of soup; dark-haired girl
- house with old woman and dead child
- Malcolm the weaver's house
- Duncan's house.

Take one of these homes each (or more than one, depending on the size of your group) and answer the following questions. Then get back together to compare answers. Between you, you should now have a detailed analysis of the whole raid through the island.

1. What happens in this incident?
2. Who or what do they encounter there?
3. How do the Vikings behave?

Discussion

You will notice that the Vikings encounter few people in this isolated community. There is the young woman who runs away, the old woman mourning a child's death, the man who ingratiates himself with them and some children. The Vikings appear almost comical, for example, when the excited dog circles them, but their potential for violence is shown in the brutal killing of the other dog. They show respect for the death of the child and appreciation for Duncan's son's wit and courage. Kol, the one despised by his comrades, is soaked, burns his mouth, gets drunk and, finally, is murdered as he lies in a drunken stupor.

Task

On your own

Using your points from the discussion above, think about the raiders and the islanders:

1. Explain how Mackay Brown builds the sense of hostility to the Vikings on the part of the islanders. In particular, think about key moments when the raiders seem to be under threat, rather than threatening.
2. Explain how Mackay Brown builds an unexpectedly human, even sympathetic, picture of the Vikings. Again, look for key moments when we are aware of this.

Discussion

1. A group of villagers, growing in size, follows them, forming a threatening presence and waiting to attack. They kill Kol. Even the old woman, grieving for the child, and Malcolm (seemingly friendly) are in this group.
2. They are not faceless marauders but very human – even sensitive. The skipper stays on board to write a poem! They react kindly to the abandoned children and are clearly Christians, not Pagans (thus, they share a belief system with the villagers). Even Kol's death does not prompt them to seek revenge: they prefer to reach the safety of the ship.

Themes

The tartan of the title is both a symbol (of Scotland/island strength) and an item of practical use: a piece of cloth to keep someone warm. The Vikings plan to give it to Kol's widow, as compensation for his loss. There is even a suggestion that she will be better off with the tartan to keep her warm and smart than she was with a useless husband like Kol.

What is Mackay Brown revealing about the community which is represented by the tartan? Is the tartan used to pull the people together in a 'Hollywood-style' defence of their homeland? The answer has to be No. In this community, we see a range of real behaviours from flawed humanity when faced with the crisis of the raid.

With a partner or in small groups

This story is interesting because of what the Vikings do **not** find as well as what they do find. Here are some questions to consider:

1. What did most of the adults do when they knew the Vikings were coming? What do you think of this?
2. Why do you think the old woman stayed behind?
3. Duncan's children are alone in their croft. What is your reaction to this?
4. Malcolm the weaver is the only adult male the Vikings meet on the island. What is your opinion of him and how did Mackay Brown help create this opinion?

Discussion

The settlement is deserted, as nearly all the adults have abandoned it: you might view this as either cowardly or sensible. The old woman is watching over the dead child and Duncan has left his children with no protection (imagine if the Vikings had been the ruthless killers of stories!). Malcolm the weaver appears to make them welcome and betrays some secrets (for example, that Morag's husband is away) in order to benefit from the situation – to urge the Vikings to punish Duncan for him. Perhaps Mackay Brown is suggesting that human beings will do anything to survive – even act in decidedly non-heroic ways.

Story 6: 'The Eye of the Hurricane'

As this is the final story in the selection, you will be able to approach studying it in a more independent way. It is one of the longest of the stories chosen for the Scottish Text section. As you would expect by now, it has a clear narrative structure, a strong sense of setting and effectively drawn characters, all combining to develop theme. There is also a stylistic feature we have not seen since 'A Time to Keep': first-person narrative. There is a significant difference in that the narrator in 'The Eye of the Hurricane' is not, in a sense, the main character but an observer of that character, Captain Stevens.

The story is about the final illness of the captain, his struggle against the harshness of life and his own self-destructive urges. The narrator, Barclay, is an outsider – a Catholic in a predominantly Church of Scotland community – who has an interested, if slightly patronising, attitude to the islanders: 'I had come to live … among simple, uncomplicated people'. We can see that the relationship between outsider and islanders is not simply one of negative impact from the dangerous outside world. It is more complex and subtle than that.

With a partner

Read the opening section up to '… corn flour and grated cheese'. Note down your first impressions of the following:

- Narrative: what tension is created between Captain Stevens, Barclay and Miriam?
- Characters: first impressions of the main character Captain Stevens and the narrator, Barclay.
- Setting: what might this contribute to the story?

Possible answers

- **Narrative:** Captain Stevens is linked to alcohol and Miriam to abstention. Barclay is in between, with his modest cans of export.
- **Characters:** Captain Stevens dominates and manipulates others. There are many examples: 'I'm rather ill' – persistent/simple demanding statement of his needs (a lie); 'don't want to interrupt' – appearing to be reasonable but actually interrupting; 'would it be too much' – suggests a minor favour/unreasonable to refuse; repetition of 'very heavy cold' to justify request. Barclay lives a simple, precise life; aims to fulfil Christian duty of charity; dedicated to writing; creature of regular habits.
- **Setting:** the island setting is further narrowed to a small town and still further to Captain Stevens's house, where much of the action will take place. Note that Captain Stevens, as Barclay's landlord, can exert influence over his actions.

Now read the rest of this story.

In small groups

Here are some activities to deepen your confident knowledge of the story and develop your analysis skills.

- Narrative: break down the narrative into the four stages you are familiar with: opening/normality – disruption/building tension – climax – resolution/new normality.
- Characters: starting with Captain Stevens, make a list of personality features and find quotations to support your choices. Next, take another character each and make notes. Get back together when you have done this. Characters to examine are Barclay, Miriam, Hackland and Jansen (you can treat them as a pair), and Captain Falquist (who appears courtesy of Captain Stevens's stories).
  As well as understanding how Mackay Brown has created each character, try to work out why each is important to the story: how he, she or they contribute to Captain Stevens's story and fate.
- Setting: consider which features of the island setting – the small port of Hamnavoe – contribute most significantly to the story.
- Theme: one important theme is the struggle for frail and flawed humanity to find fulfilment and meaning in a harsh world. You know the story well by now and will be able to comment on how the features you have already dealt with develop this theme.

Discussion

The narrative builds up to the climax of Captain Stevens's death, after which Bill watches a glowing Miriam singing of 'the storms of life' with the Salvation Army. Captain Stevens dominates the story, a charismatic yet deeply flawed character, full of grand thoughts on courage and love. The quiet, unassuming Barclay contrasts with him: note Barclay's shame about feeling sexually attracted to Miriam, whose purity provides the moral compass of the story. Hackland and Jansen are jovial but destructive side-kicks, who reveal a deeper picture of the captain, as does his memory of the romantic dreamer Falquist. The setting provides, as well as realism, the symbolism of the voyage of life and the 'eye of the hurricane' itself: a moment of quiet in life's storm.

In small groups

- Choose a section of the story.
- Make up STQ-type analysis questions on this section. (Remember, you need 10 marks spread across shorter analysis questions, and a final 10-mark question which 'goes beyond' this specific story.)
- Make up answers for each of your questions (look back at the example on pages 59 and 60 to help you).
- Have a go at answering another group's questions and then check their answers, as they check yours.

This is an excellent way of working out what sort of answers you should aim to give in your exam.

In small groups

Finally, make links between the stories. Divide up the following tasks and get back together to discuss them.

To build up your confident knowledge of the links between the stories:

- Go back to the list of themes at the start of this chapter (page 43). Make notes on which stories link with which themes.
- Look again at the diagram on 'island life' at the start of this chapter. Make notes on how the different stories demonstrate these aspects of island life.
- Characters: using the comparison approach earlier in this chapter ('A Time to Keep' and 'The Whaler's Return'), look for links between the types of characters and their experiences.
- Style/structure, for example build-up of tension and first-person narrative. Find as many 'technique' links as you can between the stories.

Possible answers

Themes

- Harsh, uncompromising nature: 'A Time to Keep', 'The Whaler's Return', 'The Bright Spade', 'The Eye of the Hurricane'.
- Community and the individual: all of them.
- Community versus the outside world: all of them.
- Tradition and progress: 'The Wireless Set', 'The Bright Spade', 'A Time to Keep', 'The Eye of the Hurricane'.
- Life and death: all of them.
- Flawed humanity finding meaning/fulfilment: all of them.

Island life

The majority of these aspects of island life feature in most of the stories, though the emphasis might be different.

Characters

Compare, for example: Bill/Flaws/Captain Stevens/Howie/Jacob/Malcolm the Weaver/Kol.

Style/structure

- Build up of suspense occurs in all of them.
- The motif of a journey appears in all of them (in 'A Time to Keep' it is a journey through time, not space).
- The 'pared down', apparently unemotional style creates greater impact.
- Although first-person narrative is only used in two examples, we are led close to the thoughts of the main characters in the other stories.

POETRY
BY ROBERT BURNS

Scotland is in the happy position of having as its national bard a world-class poet whose works have travelled successfully across national boundaries, who was an inspirational (if very human) person, and who has – generation after generation – maintained his popularity with young and old. However, you may well ask yourself: how is it possible to bring a fresh viewpoint to the works of a cultural icon?

In fact, Burns is one of the most accessible of poets – one who invites a personal response despite changes and losses, both in the Scots language and in our way of life since the eighteenth century. He wrote with a love of life, with warmth – affectionate or angry – and with breathtaking brilliance.

The six Robert Burns poems you will study for the Scottish Text section are:

- 'To a Mouse'
- 'Holy Willie's Prayer'
- 'A Poet's Welcome to his Love-Begotten Daughter'
- 'Address to the Deil'
- 'Tam o' Shanter'
- 'A Man's a Man for A' That'.

This is a rich and varied selection, dealing with a number of themes such as:

- social justice and responsibility
- hypocrisy, especially religious
- the need to live life to the full
- the need to be yourself
- rejection of life-denying attitudes.

Burns's poems are complex and this chapter cannot cover everything about every single one. Instead, the aim is to give an overview of each poem and then focus closely on specific stanzas. That way you will build your confident knowledge and analytical skills to help you study all six poems in preparation for the Higher exam.

Poem 1: 'To a Mouse'

You may know this poem and the story behind it already: a field mouse is disturbed during a late autumn ploughing and scampers off as the poet ponders why wild creatures fear human beings. In a dramatic change of focus, the mouse's true plight is revealed: its winter shelter has been destroyed by the plough. The poem moves towards a conclusion where the fate of the mouse is compared to that of humans.

Task

With a partner

Read over the following summary of the poem as it will help consolidate what you know already.

- Stanzas 1 and 2: a mouse is startled and the ploughman (the poem's speaker) apologises.
- Stanza 3: the ploughman accepts that a mouse around the farm will take its tiny share of the crop, but that's all right.
- Stanza 4: the ploughman suddenly spots that the mouse's nest has been destroyed by the plough, and there is no material for rebuilding.
- Stanzas 5 and 6: the ploughman thinks about what the mouse had planned, how hard it had worked, and what it must now face.
- Stanza 7: the ploughman realises that plans, whether made by a mouse – to whom he now feels very close in spirit – or a human, can prove useless.
- Stanza 8: the ploughman, very gloomily indeed, sees little good in his past and no hope in his future. Luckily for it, the mouse cannot look ahead anxiously.

In 'To a Mouse' tone is modulated with great skill. The poem's focus keeps changing as Burns moves it along and the tone matches these changes, intensifying from its bright start towards melancholy at the end.

Here is a list of tones which you should try to match to these stanzas:

A. Two stanzas together full of imaginative empathy.
B. Two stanzas together which seek to reassure and comfort, at first patronisingly, as if to a child, then more reflectively.
C. One stanza of fellow-feeling and identification.
D. One stanza of understanding and tolerance.
E. One stanza of despairing personal pessimism.
F. One stanza expressing a sense of shocked, guilty discovery.

Stanzas	1 and 2	3	4	5 and 6	7	8
Tone						

Possible answers

Stanzas	1 and 2	3	4	5 and 6	7	8
Tone	B	D	F	A	C	E

Spotlight on ... Persona

Tempting though it is to do so, the storyteller/narrative voice/speaker in all these poems should never be taken simply as Burns himself. Even in very personal poems there is selection and dramatisation, and the person speaking is a version of the poet. 'To a Mouse' helped create the public image of Burns as the 'simple ploughman'. He spent some of his time ploughing, but he was an educated farmer with his own equipment. There is truth in the ploughman image, but it is a heightened, dramatised truth.

Now let's examine a short extract from the poem, trying to establish the sort of ideas and details of technique on which a Scottish text question may focus.

Look at stanzas 4, 5 and 6 to examine tone more fully.

> Thy wee bit housie, too, in ruin!
> It's silly wa's the win's are strewin!
> An naethin, now, to big a new ane,
>   O foggage green!
> An bleak December's winds ensuing,
>   Baith snell an' keen!
>
> Thou saw the fields laid bare an' waste,
> An' weary winter comin' fast,
> An' cozie here beneath the blast,
>   Thou thought to dwell –
> Till crash! The cruel coulter past
>   Out thro' thy cell.
>
> That wee bit heap o' leaves an' stibble
> Has cost thee monie a weary nibble!
> Now thou's turn'd out, for a' thy trouble,
>   But house or hald,
> To thole the winter's sleety dribble,
>   And cranreuch cauld!

With a partner or in small groups

Stanza 4

1. Find two ways in which a tone of shocked realisation is created in this stanza.
2. Describe how vowel sounds help to emphasise atmosphere in the final two lines.

Stanza 5

3. Find two ways in which a tone of empathetic insight is created in this stanza.
4. How is rhythm used to emphasise this tone in the stanza?

Stanza 6

5. Give two examples (with explanations) that show word choice underlining the tone of empathy in this stanza.
6. How do the final two lines of this stanza, taken together, enhance the sense of empathy?

Possible answers

1. A series of exclamations, helping to dramatise moments when the speaker sees, then quickly understands, just what he has done. The final exclamation reveals the speaker's perception of the mouse's future – the powerful understatement where the mouse's likely fate (death from exposure) is unmentioned but left to our imagination.

2. Assonance (matching vowel sounds) connects key sounds, evoking harshness of winter: 'bleak … keen', 'December's … ensuing … snell'. The 'e' of 'snell' is a particularly hard-edged vowel sound, although the 'ea' of 'bleak' mirrors the sound used in the final stanza to create a mood of pessimism.

3. 'Thou saw' and 'Thou thought' take us into the mouse's mindset, showing us that the speaker is very aware of its standpoint.

   The last two lines of this stanza dramatise the moment when the nest was destroyed – from the mouse's viewpoint. Humans do not hear a 'crash' from a plough. Onomatopoeia, alliteration and 'oo' assonance ('cruel', 'coulter', 'Out', 'thro') underline the dramatic impact.

4. The rhythm flows regularly in the first three rhyming lines, building up descriptions and contrasts through the linking 'an': 'an' waste, / An' weary winter … / An' cozie here …'. The flow is disrupted by pause after 'dwell' and exclamation 'Till crash!', heightening our awareness of this disastrous moment. Remember Scots pronunciation: 'English' spelling can mask Scots sounds, for example 'Thoo thocht tae dwell', 'Oot throo thy cell', 'wast'.

5. 'That wee bit heap … / … monie a weary nibble!' both indicate the effort the little creature has put into creating this flimsy structure.

   '… sleety dribble, / And cranreuch cauld!' use onomatopoeia and/or alliteration to help capture the continuing misery or harshness of winter conditions.

   'thole' brings out a sense of endurance, of simply trying to survive the immediate future.

6. In an emphatic, clinching way, the last two lines bring the stanza's description of winter to a climax, providing a tragic comparison to the hard work of the mouse described at the start.

Verse form

This part is very technical, but it is helpful to learn about verse form in order to gain those extra marks.

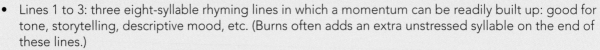

Spotlight on … The Standard Habbie

As a major element of Burns's writing, this six-line stanza form is worth taking time to understand. With stanza 5 in front of you, read on. The Standard Habbie has the following features:

- Lines 1 to 3: three eight-syllable rhyming lines in which a momentum can be readily built up: good for tone, storytelling, descriptive mood, etc. (Burns often adds an extra unstressed syllable on the end of these lines.)
- Lines 4 and 6: two four-syllable lines that rhyme only with each other. These can be snappy, but the snappiness can be used for understatement, introducing a thoughtful, reflective note. If there appear to be more syllables on the written page, this is because, when reading aloud, it would only be four.
- Line 5: sandwiched between lines 4 and 6 is one line of eight syllables, rhyming with the first 3.
- Lines 4, 5 and 6 can be used simply as a climax, but they can also turn the mood, introduce a note of irony or satire, or bring in a surprise or an aside.

Spotlight on ... Rhythm and rhyme

The basic rhythm Scots- and English-language poets use tends to be **iambic rhythm**, as in:

ti	TUM	ti	TUM	ti	TUM	ti	TUM
'Thou	SAW	the	FIELDS	laid	BARE	an'	WASTE'

It is a 'rising' rhythm that ensures the line ends on a definite closing beat, a stress.

When the line ends on an unstressed syllable, as in 'beastie', 'breastie' or 'hasty', this can be referred to as a feminine ending or **feminine rhyme**. Oddly enough, it seems well suited to anger, humour and gentleness. If the whole line is taken over by this, the rhythm becomes:

TUM ti TUM ti TUM ti TUM ti

which is a 'falling' or cadential rhythm.

This is now **trochaic rhythm**, composed of four trochaic 'feet', to which the first line of the poem comes close:

TUM	TUM ti	TUM ti	TUM ti	TUM ti
WEE	SLEEkit	COW'rin	TIM'rous	BEASTie

When Burns uses feminine rhyme, he might bring in some trochaic feet to support tone or mood. Trochaic rhythm's downbeat characteristic, again, seems to suit it to the emotional range noted above and can also help create a sense of swift-flowing lines.

With a partner

The poem's opening stanza seeks to reassure the mouse. Its tone is caring, in a gently patronising, parent-to-slightly-hurt-child way. Look again at this stanza. How does Burns create this tone, looking at the following?

(a) rhyme
(b) rhythm

Possible answers

(a) Feminine rhyme is used throughout the stanza, helping to indicate cheerful tenderness (especially as it incorporates 'childish' word forms such as 'beastie' and 'breastie', pronounced 'breestie').

(b) The opening list of adjectives to describe its fearful state creates trochaic 'falling' rhythm, which contributes to a reassuring effect. This comforting tone is developed by the gentle exclamation in line 2.

The poem as comment on the human condition

After the opening address, stanza 2 is more apologetic and rapidly becomes an opportunity for the narrator to reflect on more abstract issues – apparently about human and animal relationships, though with radical politics mixed in. This was a time when ideas of social justice and equality were spreading through Europe.

The opening sense of gentleness prepares the way for the deeper involvement that emerges in stanzas 4 to 6, when the ploughman realises that this is no mere disturbance but a destruction of the nest – a likely death sentence.

Task

With a partner

1. Discuss how empathy becomes full-on fellow-feeling in stanza 7.
2. Discuss why the ploughman's own troubles become the focus of stanza 8.

Possible answers

1. Empathy becomes fellow-feeling in stanza 7 when the ploughman realises that the mouse's shattered plans to survive the winter are similar to the failure of human foresight: 'the best-laid schemes' can fare no better.

2. He now thinks of his own failed plans and the burden of the 'prospects drear' of his own past, and then of a future about which he can only 'guess an' fear'. This sets the final, melancholic, pessimistic tone.

If a Scottish Text question or Critical Essay question asks how Burns's poetry relates to social conditions, the mouse could be seen as symbolic of the plight of those folk who lived on the soil at that time: the more work and improvement small tenant farmers like Burns put into their land, the more danger they were in of increased, unpayable rents and eviction. They were also hugely at the mercy of bad weather, and the mid-1780s were awful.

Therefore, the poem becomes an allegory of human problems:

- stanzas 2 and 3 seem decidedly political
- stanzas 4, 5 and 6 deal with the hardships
- stanzas 7 and 8 move from allegory or fable into straightforwardly human subject matter.

Links with other poems

If you have read other Burns poems on the list, try this activity. If not, leave it till later.

The final 10-mark question in the Scottish text questions asks you to look at what your given poem has in common with at least one other (commonality). This question might refer to themes, aspects, issues emerging from the selected stanzas, or stylistic links such as tone, atmosphere or verse form. Which poems might link in with 'To a Mouse'?

Poem 2: 'Holy Willie's Prayer'

This poem is one of the world's great examples of an auto-destructive dramatic monologue. The lack of self-knowledge, the hubris (overblown pride) and petty vindictiveness that Willie expresses in his prayer condemn him as a fool and a hypocrite, and also gave us the term 'Holy Willie' for all such as he.

Burns's satire here was turned against William Fisher, the prototype of Willie, who was one of the Kirk of Scotland's Auld Licht group. Auld Lichters saw God as a condemnatory deity, who was not at all impressed by kind deeds but exercised an arbitrary system of Grace to choose who was hell-bound and who was 'saved' for heaven. Burns was a practising Christian but he hated this powerful sect. Fall-outs with them were regular: it was personal.

One of the interesting things in the progress of his 'prayer' is seeing how Willie tries to deal with the essentials of a prayer to God before moving on to his prayer's real reason: his desire for revenge.

With a partner

Having read the poem, try these questions to allow you to focus on the structure and some of the detail of this fine piece of satirical irony.

1. Stanzas 1 to 6 seem to be dedicated to praising God.
   (a) How many of these stanzas are also about Willie?
   (b) From one of these stanzas, quote a short extract which shows that Willie's God does not demonstrate kindness and forgiveness.
2. Stanzas 7 to 11 form a plea for forgiveness.
   (a) In how many of these stanzas does Willie seek to justify, excuse or strike a bargain about his sins?
   (b) From one of these stanzas, quote an extract which suggests that Willie is a sexual predator.
3. Stanzas 12 to 17 proclaim Willie's desire for revenge.
   (a) How many of these stanzas seem to show Willie's anxiety about his public image and reputation?
   (b) From one of these stanzas, find a two-line quotation in which Burns ridicules Willie by showing us his pettiness. Then find another two-line quotation in which Burns appals us with a picture of Willie's vindictiveness.
4. Look again at the structure of the final stanza and comment on what it tells us about Willie's relationship with his God.

Possible answers

1. (a) Five.
   (b) 'As it pleases best Thysel / Sends ane to Heaven an' ten to Hell', *or*
   '... thousands Thou hast left in night', *or*
   '... damnation / For broken laws, / Six thousand years 'ere my creation', *or*
   'When from my mither's womb I fell, / Thou might hae plung'd me deep in hell'
2. (a) Four.
   (b) 'Wi' Leezie's lass, three times I trow – / But Lord, that Friday I was fou / When I cam near her', *or*
   'Maybe Thou lets this fleshly thorn / Buffet Thy servant e'en an morn'
3. (a) Four.
   (b) **Willie's pettiness:** 'curse Thou his basket and his store, / Kail an' potatoes'
   Willie's vindictiveness: 'But for Thy people's sake destroy them, / An' dinnae spare'
4. Willie's needs and demands occupy four lines, showing that he expects personal care and material benefits from God. His parting one-line of praise for God simply demonstrates his smugness.

With a partner

Read again stanzas 4, 5 and 6. The focus is on the satirical impact of Burns's writing, which, in this poem, is vital.

1. In stanza 4, how does Burns ridicule the superstitious nature of Willie's belief?
2. How does Burns use hyperbole (intentional exaggeration) and symbolism in stanza 5 to undermine Willie's hubris (overwhelming pride)?
3. Burns wrote poetry suited to reading aloud (and, in many cases, singing, of course). This fostered his love of sound techniques, perhaps particularly assonance. Can you detect how Burns uses sound in stanza 6 to emphasise the ridiculousness of Willie's behaviour and views? (Remember that the correct Scots pronunciation in this stanza is 'sw**ee**rers' and 'sw**ee**r'.)

Possible answers

1. Simply being born is linked to Adam and Eve's 'fall' from Eden: '... from my mither's womb I fell'.

   The ludicrous image of a newborn baby 'gnashing' its gums in hell – where this monstrous God has 'plung'd' it.

   The use of final three lines of stanza 4 conjure up a medieval vision of hell, with lots of roaring and yelling.

2. Christianity is the religion of humility, so Willie's attitude is un-Christian.

   The suggestion that Willie can actually demonstrate something as huge as God's grace.

   '... pillar o' Thy temple, / Strong as a rock' – these are basic symbols of the Christian Church. Willie thinks he has achieved St Peter's status simply by being 'here'.

3. Strong word 'zeal' (enthusiasm – seen then as sign of religious extremism) echoes throughout the stanza in all other 'ee' words.

   Assonance ('ee') climaxes on 'Thy fear' – this emphasises the miserable view of God, obeyed only through fear of hell.

On your own or with a partner

In stanzas 4, 5 and 6, Burns mocks Willie's belief that newborn babies can go straight to hell. Using your knowledge and analytic skills, look at how Burns's scathing view of Willie's religion is developed elsewhere in the poem. Choose two stanzas for this.

Possible answers

Stanza 13
- Word choice 'chasten'd': Willie's understatement for self-righteous bullying.
- Lines 2, 3 and 4: tone of complaint (spoilt child to indulgent parent).
- Bathos (the unlikely descent from serious to ridiculous): 'Curse Thou his basket and his store, / Kail an' potatoes'. 'Curse Thou' is serious; 'potatoes' less so.
- Burns mocks Willie for complaining about being mocked.

Stanza 16
- Context: having inveigled himself into God's favour, Willie now demands his side of the bargain.
- There is a series of commands to God, one per line. He remembers to say 'Lord' in the first two lines, then piles on demands. 'And', 'Nor' and 'But' keep the vindictiveness flowing.
- Note how he closes loopholes of 'mercy' and 'pray'r'.
- Rhyme scheme: sermon-like repetitiveness as Willie hammers away and rhyme/repetition picks this up: 'try him' / 'employ him' / 'by them' / 'destroy them'.
- Feminine rhyme helps to convey spite and nastiness.

> You will see a lot is crammed into each stanza. Remember, Burns was a genius!

Links with other poems

Scottish Text questions

Read stanzas 1 to 7 again and then tackle these analysis questions. The final question asks you to link 'Holy Willie's Prayer' to other poems, so you may need to come back to this later.

1. Analyse how, in these stanzas, Burns uses ideas and language to demonstrate that Willie is motivated by self-interest. **4**
2. Burns rejects the version of God that Willie chose to believe in. Analyse how Burns uses language to make this clear. **4**
3. Explain how Burns uses the Standard Habbie verse form to intensify his ridicule/criticism of Willie. **2**
4. The use of humour – in one of its many varieties – is a feature of much of Burns's writing. By referring to this and at least one other poem, discuss how humour is used as a key element. (Note: you will be able to answer this question more readily if you have read the other poems.) **10**

Possible answers

1. A prayer to God, but after stanza 1 Willie's special place in 'Thy [God's] sight' is emphasised time after time – until he instructs God on why he should forgive him: 'But Thou remembers we are dust, / Defil'd wi' sin'.

   Willie is 'A burning and a shining light'. Word choice suggests he is God's weapon against sinners ('burning') and an inspiration to all ('shining'). This is due to God's 'matchless might' providing Willie with 'gifts an' grace' (God's power/generosity emphasised by alliteration) and implication is that this generosity should continue.

   2 marks for a detailed/insightful comment plus a quotation/reference. 1 mark for a more basic comment plus a quotation/reference. 0 marks for a quotation with no comment. Total: 4 marks. (Marks can be gained 2+2, 2+1+1 or 1+1+1+1.)

2. Emphasis on ridiculous proportion of sinners to saved: 'Sends ane to Heaven an' ten to Hell'. Willie is blessed 'When thousands Thou hast left in night'.

   Image of newborn child being (potentially) immediately condemned: 'When from my mither's womb I fell' – 'fell' suggests the fall into sin – baby in hell illustrated graphically: 'To gnash my gums, and weep and wail, / In burnin lakes'. Picture of a toothless baby juxtaposed with that of horrendous torture.

   Stanza 6 is dominated by key words 'zeal' and 'fear', linked by the 'ee' assonance found in five lines – implies Willie's enthusiasm is founded on fear.

   2 marks for a detailed/insightful comment plus a quotation/reference. 1 mark for a more basic comment plus a quotation/reference. 0 marks for a quotation with no comment. Total: 4 marks. (Marks can be gained 2+2, 2+1+1 or 1+1+1+1.)

3. In stanza 5, Willie builds up a vision of himself through the first three lines. Feminine rhyme helps suggest that he is mesmerised by these boasts, then the fourth is a monosyllabic short line 'Strong as a rock' – the contrast should bring to mind Christ's praise of his disciple Peter as his Rock, on which to build the Church.

   2 marks for a detailed/insightful comment plus a quotation/reference. 1 mark for a more basic comment plus a quotation/reference. 0 marks for a quotation with no comment. Total: 2 marks. (Marks can be gained 2 or 1+1.)

→

4. **Up to 2 marks for a general explanation of how Burns uses humour in his poems (commonality). For example:**

When celebrating what is good in life, or attacking injustice and hypocrisy, Burns uses humour to help express his viewpoint. This varies from biting irony to more cheerful forms of hyperbole and wordplay.

Up to 2 marks for comments on this section. For example:

In 'Holy Willie's Prayer', Burns uses sustained irony to present Willie as a ridiculous, laughable self-deluder who feels he is doing God's work by interfering: 'When drinkers drink an' swearers swear, / An' singin' here, an' dancin' there'. This presents a comical picture of a self-righteous busybody.

3 x 2 marks for comments and references from other poems, of which there are many. Here are some examples:

- 'Address to the Deil' takes his view of Willie's hell a stage further – here the Devil 'spairges about the brunstane cootie, / To scaud poor wretches' – the impression of the Devil being either so enthusiastic or so short-handed that he does hands-on torturing himself, with his 'cootie' (small pail) and brimstone.
- 'Tam o' Shanter': the Devil turns up as the piper at witches' dance: a comical figure of 'a towsie tyke [big dog], black, grim and large'. Excited by Nannie's beauty, but sublimates this in musical efforts: 'Ev'n Satan glowr'd, and fidg'd fu fain / And hotch'd and blew wi' might and main'.
- Portrayal of Tam himself contributes to comicality: the hero, but only 'heroic' because of drink, and only just: he gallops onwards 'Whiles glow'ring round wi prudent cares / Lest bogles catch him unawares'. His horse Maggie is much more sensible – keen to avoid Kirk Alloway – and finally she is the true hero: 'Ae spring brought off her master hale'.   **Total: 10 marks.**

Poem 3: 'Address to the Deil'

In this poem, the 'bogeyman' who haunted the European consciousness through the Middle Ages into the sixteenth and seventeenth centuries – where his threatening presence led to thousands of 'witchcraft' executions – and who was still warily believed in by many in Burns's own century, is turned by Burns into a mock-serious figure of fun. How does he construct the 'fun'?

Look at structure again, and be aware of Burns's love of old folk tales and his pleasure – though not belief – in folk superstitions. We can then ask how he manipulates tradition to create a sense of irreverent comedy.

Task

With a partner or in small groups

Read the descriptions below and match each stanza to a description. They are in the correct order but most descriptions contain more than one stanza.

A. Haranguing the Devil, using various folk names to get him to pause in his activities and listen to this address.
B. A slightly more respectful summary of what is supposed to be the Devil's habitual behaviour when not in hell.
C. Scary moments given a satanic interpretation, thanks to the idea of a 'Deil' who operates at a very local level.
D. Witchcraft and its effect in local businesses and travel safety.
E. One rather mystifying stanza relating to a strangely dangerous ritual.
F. Familiar biblical tales of the Devil's doings.
G. One stanza about the sheer scale of the Devil's doings.
H. Personal, quite interactive stanzas with a twist of pathos.

Description	A	B	C	D	E	F	G	H
Stanza(s)								

Description	A	B	C	D	E	F	G	H
Stanza(s)	1 and 2	3 and 4	5, 6, 7 and 8	9, 10, 11, 12 and 13	14	15, 16, 17 and 18	19	20 and 21

Humour

The spirit of comedy can sometimes fail dismally to transfer from decade to decade, let alone across centuries – besides which we all have our individual sense of humour. What continues to surprise new readers of Burns is how his direct, disrespectful approach can transport a freshness of wit and irony from past to present.

The questions below are based on stanza 1:

> O Thou! whatever title suit thee!
> Auld Hornie, Satan, Nick, or Clootie,
> Wha in yon cavern grim an' sooty
>   Clos'd under hatches,
> Spairges about the brunstane cootie,
>   To scaud poor wretches!

Task

With a partner or in small groups

1. Can you explain the immediate ironic irreverence (over-familiarity, cheek) of the opening two lines?
2. In what way is the word 'sooty' undermining? (Hint: think about all houses in Burns's time – open fireplaces, peat or coal fires.)
3. How does line 4 trivialise hell?
4. In line 5, the Devil is splashing around brimstone from a little pail. Can you explain the comicality of this?
5. How does the expression 'poor wretches' undermine the idea of what hell is all about? Think back to Holy Willie's view of those in hell.
6. What part does the rhyme play in keeping the ironically humorous tone going?
7. Comment on how the rhythm contributes to the feel of this stanza. Think back to 'To a Mouse' and remember trochaic rhythm and its links to feminine rhyme.

1. 'O Thou!' and 'title' seem serious, but the invitation to choose his own title is disparaging. The list of mostly undignified names further undermines his status, especially 'Clootie' (reference to hooves).

2. Very homely (cottars' houses all had layers of soot) – far from 'grim'.

3. A hell that can be concealed under 'hatches' seems small-scale and diminished – bathos at work.

4. Imagine the Prince of Darkness doing the bucket work himself!

5. No sense of sinners suffering deserved punishment – they are just unfortunate souls. Compare this with Holy Willie's approval of hell.

6. Feminine rhyme throughout: the rhythm seems to tumble from line to line, keeping mock-serious insolence rolling along.

7. Trochaic rhythm dominates most lines (feminine rhyme contributing); falling rhythm is put to comical use: '... cavern **grim** an' **sooty**', '... **brun**stane **coot**ie'.

With a partner

Choose either stanza 13 or stanza 20. Find three aspects of content or language (or a mixture) which seem aimed at creating a comical, light-hearted or ironic effect. Once you have noted down some ideas, join with another pair to make a group and share ideas.

Possible answers

Stanza 13

- Gullible persona: accepts supernatural explanation of 'Spunkies' without question.
- Feminine rhyme: with deliberately awkward 'drunk is … sunk is'.
- 'Spunkies', 'mischievous monkies': noticeable rhymes emphasise silly terms for murderous devils. Dark humour, as people die in these bogs.
- Bathos of line 3: serious invective, then 'monkies'.
- 'miry slough': posh way to say 'bog'.

Stanza 20

- Cheeky familiarity of 'auld Cloots'.
- Comical view of the 'Bardie' (poet) outwitting the Devil.
- Cheerful self-deprecation of 'A certain Bardie's rantin, drinkin'.
- '… he'll turn a corner jinkin [dodging]': excellent metaphor for vaguely hopeful defiance.
- Pointless antagonising of the Devil in the promise to 'cheat' him – of what should be his!

The use of tone in stanzas 20 and 21 is particularly effective. The whole poem is ironic: there is a thin layer of superficial seriousness expressed through the persona of the speaker, who is really quite foolish: gullible one moment and defying the Devil the next. He is unsure just how to approach the Devil, but sees avoiding his traps as a kind of game. His tone is perhaps one of uneasy bravado, but then suddenly, in the final stanza, compassion breaks through in the persona's sympathy for the Devil. Burns often shows sympathy for flawed humanity and here the Devil is only human.

Poem 4: 'A Poet's Welcome to his Love-Begotten Daughter'

This is a brilliant piece of work, which comes across as spontaneous, impassioned and 'unplanned' but which actually demonstrates sophisticated and innovative skills in persona creation and intermingling of tones. Its daring honesty has made it a firm favourite over the years: it takes on the stern Presbyterian Auld Licht condemnation of sex out of wedlock (a major offence in the eighteenth century) to celebrate this out-of-wedlock bairn.

With a partner or in small groups

Match the following stanza descriptions to the appropriate stanzas. They are not in order.

A. A promise to provide a decent upbringing – she will be well dressed and go to school (even if he is hard up).
B. A statement of defiance where he insists that he is not bothered what they say. In fact, he shows real contempt for anyone wishing to criticise.
C. A prayer for her future – hoping she turns out a lot like her mother and a bit like her father.
D. Here the father says, 'Hello,' before rapidly promising he will never be ashamed of her. Contains very sweet parent–child expressions.
E. A very tender first line – and then an admission that she certainly was not planned and that he has had problems with the Church.
F. A fatherly promise to give her good advice – which he hopes she will listen to – and then a fine positive pledge.
G. He remembers the conception cheerfully, then seems to be a bit troubled and returns to financial responsibility.
H. A warm, affectionate stanza towards mother as well as daughter, although there is a harsh change of tone at the end.

Description	A	B	C	D	E	F	G	H
Stanza								

Possible answers

Description	A	B	C	D	E	F	G	H
Stanza	5	2	7	1	3	8	4	6

With a partner or in small groups

Let us look at the poem's emotional pattern or structure. Group the stanzas in this way:

A. Stanzas that are mostly negative, on the attack or sarcastic.
B. Stanzas that are more or less balanced and include both positive and negative.
C. Stanzas that are mostly positive: celebratory, accepting, etc.

Emotional pattern	A	B	C
Stanza			

Possible answers

Emotional pattern	A	B	C
Stanza	2	3, 4 and 6	1, 5, 7 and 8

This shows us that the father is quick to go on the attack against community disapproval, but is soon drawn back towards more tender emotions that dominate as the poem ends.

Let us look at some of Burns's favoured techniques at work in stanza 2.

Tho' now they ca' me **fornicator**,
An **t**ease my name in **k**intry **clatter** [pronounced 'claitter'],
The mair they **t**alk, I'm **k**ent the b**etter**,
      E'en let them **clash**;
An **auld wife's t**ongue's a **feckless matter** [pronounced 'maitter']
      To gie ane **fash**.

Feminine rhyme (lines 1 to 3 and 5) – in this case supporting a contemptuous, ridiculing tone.

Word choice: dismissive, insulting words add to the tone: 'clash', 'feckless', 'auld wife's' and 'fash'.

Sound: patterns of alliteration and consonance help to strengthen the tone: c's, cl's and t's all emphasise words of contempt or defiance.

As well as echoing through the rhymes, the stanza's key word – the accusation the speaker is defying: 'fornicator' – is picked up in the defiant f's at the end.

Structure: the last two lines of the stanza add the final defiant twist: an effective feature of the Standard Habbie (their gossip will not 'fash' (bother) him).

Now look again at stanza 7, which has a very different tone from stanza 2.

Lord grant that thou may aye inherit
Thy mither's person, grace, an' merit,
An' thy poor, worthless daddy's spirit,
      Without his failins,
'Twill please me mair to see thee heir it,
      Than stockit mailens.

Task

With a partner or in small groups

1. Which words instil a religious, heightened tone?
2. In lines 2 and 3, how does Burns create a contrast?
3. What is the effect of feminine rhyme in this case? (Hint: the opposite of stanza 2.)
4. What does the structure of the Standard Habbie contribute?

Possible answers

1. 'Lord grant', 'thou', 'grace' and 'thy'.

2. A list of the mother's qualities is compared favourably to a short list of adjectives criticising the father, from which 'spirit' emerges positively.

3. It adds a gentle, encouraging quality that ties in with the religious mood and sense of a blessing.

4. The four positive lines containing what he wants for his child (personal virtues) are balanced by two stating what he does not value so highly for her (material wealth).

Now look again at stanza 5.

> Tho' I should be the waur bestead,
> Thou's be as braw and bienly clad,
> And thy young years as nicely bred
> Wi' education,
> As ony brat o' wedlock's bed,
> In a' thy station.

On your own or with a partner

Identify the techniques used to convey the theme of responsibility and comment on how they are used. (Hint: look for contrast, alliteration and rhyme.)

Possible answers

- Structure: four positive, serious lines, pledging the father's care; contrast with defiance in final lines – this will happen whatever people say.
- Alliteration on 'b' and 'br' consonants, adding a sense of punchy determination.
- Solid masculine rhyme (that is, one stressed syllable rhyming): hard 'e' vowels and strong 'd' consonants stating his pledge. ('Clad' is pronounced 'cled' in Scots.)
- Be aware of the place of this stanza in the structure of the poem – after this, the tone maintains its seriousness as the father seems to grow into a considered acceptance of his new role.

Links with other poems

On your own or with a partner

This task asks you to link 'A Poet's Welcome to his Love-Begotten Daughter' to other poems, so you may need to come back to this later.

Consider the poem's theme of disapproving and intrusive moral or religious attitudes towards unmarried parents. How does this link with the following poems?

(a) 'To a Mouse'
(b) 'Holy Willie's Prayer'
(c) 'Address to the Deil'

Possible answers

- (a) 'To a Mouse': sense of poverty/insecurity of life; desire for security.
- (b) 'Holy Willie's Prayer': Willie represents similar 'fundamentalist' morality – obviously an important sector of the Kirk – with strong opposition also.
- (c) 'Address to the Deil': evidence of active belief in hell and that the supernatural intrudes into everyday life.

Poem 5: 'Tam o' Shanter'

This wonderful poem is possibly Burns's most accomplished piece, containing a rich variety of ingredients, though Tam's stormy gallop is its driving force. It has a superficial 'moral', undercut by irony and other, more implicit, themes.

'Tam' has a very accessible narrative and Burns has conveniently divided it into various-sized sections for us. The breaks between these irregular 'stanzas' give the galloping reciter time to gather breath for changes in tone or pace. This poem was meant to be, was, and still is, as much oral as written literature.

It contains elements of traditional heroic journey narratives. Our hero must abandon comfort to gallop into danger. He will not avoid confrontation. He plunges from the frying pan into the fire. He narrowly escapes with his life. However, it is all mock-heroic if the end of his quest is somehow to get home safely; Tam's homecoming certainly means his 'ain wife Kate', but it also means her long-suffering fury at this 'drunken blellum' of a man's irresponsible behaviour. In terms of theme, it is worth examining the true power that the female exhibits in this apparently male viewpoint-centred tale.

Task

With a partner or in small groups

There are nineteen irregular stanzas in this poem. Start by numbering them.

1. The stanzas can be divided into ten workable sections, each of which helps create either the atmosphere or the moral of the poem. In 'atmosphere' sections, description comes through strongly. In 'moral' sections, the narrator tries to convey a message about how to behave. Look at the descriptions below and read through each section again.

   A. Stanzas 1 and 2 describe a difficulty facing country dwellers in general, Tam in particular.
   B. Stanzas 3 and 4 are about ignoring good advice in favour of alcohol.
   C. Stanzas 5 and 6 capture the essence of snug conviviality on a stormy evening.
   D. Stanza 7 admonishes us that stress-free happiness is temporary and reality will soon intervene. For Tam, reality is looking grim.
   E. Stanzas 8, 9 and 10 show a combination of hostile weather elements besetting Tam, who seems reasonably undaunted despite gruesome events that have happened there previously. Then a surprise.
   F. Stanza 11 portrays the destabilising effect of alcohol on natural caution.
   G. Stanzas 12 and 13 present an apparently enjoyable 'ceilidh from hell'.
   H. Stanzas 14, 15 and 16 provide a narrator's comment and value judgement.
   I. Stanzas 17 and 18 feature similes, a pursuit and a close thing.
   J. Stanza 19 teaches us all a lesson – or does it?

   Decide which of the above stanza sections help to create the atmosphere in the poem, and which help to create the moral of the poem, and write a list for each. **Check your answers first before moving on to tasks 2 and 3.**

This gives us some idea of Burns's storytelling strategy: in-built 'moral' moments delay the action, making us eager to find out what Tam will do next, then suddenly (at G, H and I) we are free of moral interruptions as the poem builds to its climax before the final moral parting shot.

2. Looking at the four 'moral moments' you identified in task 1, sum up what the superficial moral or message of the poem appears to be.
3. Why does it seem that this is not a serious moral theme?

Possible answers

1. **Atmosphere:** sections A, C, E, G, H, I.

   Moral: sections B, D, F, J.

2. Husband who ignores wife's advice – especially where alcohol is concerned – is an irresponsible fool.

   The pleasures of alcohol, sexual attraction, etc. (by implication, the pleasures of life) are false, fleeting and will lead to moral and physical danger.

3. The poem is comedic – full of fantasy, exaggeration, undercutting – all presented ironically, including Tam's escape.

   The witches' dancing is the lively, energetic heart of the poem, there to enjoy, not deplore.

   Tam does escape: the final, anti-climactic message seems to be 'behave or your horse loses its tail!'

Focus on analysis of specific stanzas

Although of course the major feature of a narrative poem is the overall structure – the story's flow – we must be equally attentive to the details that give it its unique life. Burns's poetic skills are as evident here as in his more obviously theme-derived pieces. You will come across now-familiar features such as feminine rhyme, trochaic rhythm, word choice and all the sound-effects that bind and emphasise, helping to create mood. Also look out for sentence structure, particularly the use of repetition.

Task

On your own or with a partner

The great 'set scenes' of this poem are all, in a way, taken at the 'gallop'. These include Tam's ride, the dancing and the chase. Read stanza 5 again, from 'The night drave on …' to '… the storm a whistle'.

1. Can you show how this extract from the inn scene, though indoors and sedentary (Tam is 'planted'), creates the same sense of a fast pace?
2. Why do you think Burns decided on a speedy rhythm at this point?
3. Whenever Tam might appear to be doing well, Burns reminds us that he is a rather foolish chap. How does he do that in this section?
4. Find one other stanza where you see Tam's 'heroism' clearly undermined and briefly show how Burns has done this. (Hint: look at language and/or content.)

Possible answers

1. Feminine rhyme is used throughout. This creates a fast pace as the lines move rapidly into each other:

   - 'drave' suggests swift physical movement.
   - 'clatter' can mean the noise of speedy movement.
   - Sentence structure roughly repeats itself as activities rapidly accumulate: 'The night … / the ale … / The landlady … / The Souter …'.

- Trochaic rhythm is present from '... **fav**ours **sec**ret, **sweet** and **prec**ious' onwards. This creates a sense of speed.
- Alliteration, assonance and consonance in 'secret, sweet and precious'.

2. To give a sense of the night racing away, preparing us for the gallop to come.

3. 'clatter' suggests empty talk, babbling.

   'ay the ale was growing better' – very unlikely! Tam is becoming drunk.

   The landlady's behaviour suggests false intimacy with Tam to keep him buying beer.

   The landlord's laugh is suspect and Tam's bravado is drink-induced.

4. There are examples in stanzas 6, 7, 9, 10, 11, 12, 13, 14, 15, 16 and 18. Examples from stanza 11:

- Focuses on the deluding power of alcohol – described heroically as 'Inspiring, bold ...'.
- Courage is 'graded' according to strength of the drink.
- Tam's reckless courage is described with comically rhyming words: 'noddle' and 'boddle'.
- Maggie has more sense and is punished for her intelligent caution.

Spotlight on ... Narrative persona

The narrative persona – the storyteller of the poem – is a character in himself. Read over stanza 15 again to gain an insight into this. Here you see him as excited as Tam over Nannie – absorbed in telling us all about her – until, at the end of the stanza, he 'remembers' his moral message. Throughout the poem the same interplay is seen between his appreciation of Tam's story and his moral duty to warn us. Try to find other stanzas where this dual-purpose role can be seen.

Links with other poems

The final theme is all about the rich enjoyment of life. This theme determines much of what Burns writes, either as an obvious celebration or in response to the criticism of happiness and fun by gloomy folk.

Task

With a partner

1. Find a stanza where this theme emerges strongly.
2. Explain how this links to the poem as a whole.
3. Explain how your stanza could link with one or two other poems in terms of this theme. (This is useful practice for the final 10-mark question.)

Possible answers

1. Stanza 1 creates an atmosphere of communal conviviality at the end of a working day, *or*

   Stanza 9 creates a terrifying journey, but the emphasis is on Tam's breathless excitement and the momentum of the gallop.

2. A sense of warmth and entertainment is established at the start, which sets the tone for the poem, *or*

   Fast movement will transfer into the dancing scene; his foolish, drunken courage will be a catalyst.

3. 'A Poet's Welcome to his Love-Begotten Daughter': this is a celebration of a baby's birth, despite complications.

   'Address to the Deil': apparent fear of supernatural is comically undermined; old, once-harmful superstitions are transformed through humour.

Spotlight on ... Scots and English

'Tam o' Shanter' is a very rich Scots-language piece, with Burns's love of the language evident in most areas, from 'drouthy neibors', 'by an ingle' and 'smoor'd' to 'towzie tyke', 'cleekit' and 'reekit', 'cutty-sark' and 'carlin'.

The often onomatopoeic, 'gutsy' quality of many Scots words, such as the examples above, is well used here. However, it is also perhaps one of Burns's most successful pieces of English writing, famously so in stanza 7, which seems to split 50/50 on English/Scots. It seems that Burns wants us to see his narrator as someone who can 'do' English – and who will attempt it at certain moments – but who will forget to do so once the story is really under way and he is caught up in it.

Poem 6: 'A Man's a Man for A' That'

For a long time this anthemic lyric matched 'Auld Lang Syne' for universal popularity. It was the song of the struggle for democracy and human rights, directly inspired by Thomas Paine's great democratic essay of 1791, *Rights of Man*, which was banned when this poem was being written, although Burns had a copy. Even the most forward-thinking referred to humanity as 'Man' back then.

'A Man's a Man for A' That' has remained an inspirational song, although you will probably study it as a poem: beautifully balanced between bitter attack and optimistic praise. The choral phrase 'for a' that' suggests that despite all difficulties and nonsense the world throws at us, humanity and basic decency will win in the end.

You can watch two very different versions of the poem being sung on YouTube: Sheena Wellington's inspiring performance at the opening of the Scottish Parliament, and Paolo Nutini, who brings it brilliantly alive for a young audience when performing in concert.

Overview

- The first four stanzas combine disapproval and approval, each building towards a positive declaration that develops or clarifies Burns's theme, the absolute importance of real human qualities.

- All this builds towards the passionate humanist 'prayer' of the final stanza, as the poem's movement reflects that of each earlier stanza.

Task

On your own or with a partner

This multiple-choice task focuses on the structured progress of the poem. Be prepared to justify your choices. Choose the descriptions that best fit each stanza.

Stanza 1

A. The speaker attacks slavery before suggesting that money is not the most important thing in life; people are.
B. The speaker shows contempt for people who are ashamed of their own low social status before insisting that a person's true value is found within.
C. The speaker tells us not to be cowardly, but daring at all times.

Stanza 2

A. The speaker illustrates the unimportance of social status by denigrating status symbols and then declaring that human qualities provide the only true superiority.

B. The speaker emphasises the benefits of the plain, simple life over the wealthy one, then says a poor person should always be crowned king.

C. The speaker says that honest men should never wear fancy clothes.

Stanza 3

A. Being wealthy encourages people to walk and dress in a ridiculous way, which is at least entertaining to spectators.

B. The arrogance that comes with status will always be derided by people who think for themselves.

C. If you move around in a confident way, people will respect you and enjoy your jokes.

Stanza 4

A. So-called important people are dependent on the favours of those above them, unlike those who rely on their own inner qualities.

B. You are better to achieve a high ranking in society through your own efforts, not the king's influence.

C. People with titles are generally dishonest but at least they are dignified.

Stanza 5

Create your own summary sentence for this stanza. Could these lines be the most important Burns (or anyone else) ever wrote?

Possible answers

1 – B; 2 – A; 3 – B; 4 – A

Stanza 5: a message of hope that the moral qualities mentioned previously will prevail universally, leading to friendship between all peoples and nations.

In stanzas 1 and 2, the poem's theme of honesty as the quality that defines a kind of inner nobility emerges. The 'tinsel show' of wealth and power cannot match this. This theme is developed as follows:

- Foolish emptiness of nobility ridiculed in stanza 3.

- Then mocked by an honest man – 'the man o' independent mind'.

- Then the attack is upgraded to royalty ...

- ... who cannot 'make' an honest man – they have no influence on inner qualities ...

- ... which are what true 'higher rank' is all about.

- The final stanza is a prayer that fine abstract qualities will rule the world ...

- ... when honest men will all be brothers, all equal, none ruling.

'A Man's a Man for A' That' is a resounding piece of work – political, opinionated – but much more than that. At its heart it is an attack on 'inferiority': on the socially acceptable – and expected – low self-esteem of ordinary people. It urges us to believe in ourselves and to take pride in what we are, and is full of enthusiasm and hope.

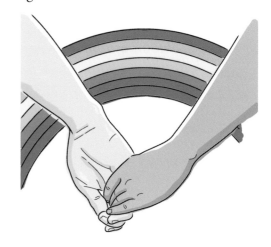

Reflect on the perfect balance between satirical invective and positive message. Think of the strong visual images that leap out in stanzas 1 to 3 and the simple but effective word choice and alliteration that strengthen these. Notice how the structures of each of stanzas 1 to 4 reflect that of the poem, as each upbeat ending builds towards the positive crescendo of the final stanza.

Using your knowledge of all the poems

With all the poems at your disposal, try the following analysis questions.

Scottish Text questions

Look again at 'Address to the Deil'. Read from stanza 15 to the end of the poem. Stanzas 15 to 18 are the poem's most biblical section, involving Adam and Eve (the 'youthfu' lovers') and Job ('the man of Uzz') who was horribly tortured by the Devil. Then try these analysis questions. For the final question, try to find as many links with the other poems as you can.

1. Look at stanzas 15 to 19. Analyse how language is used to create contrast in these lines. **4**
2. The speaker creates an informal, disrespectful tone when speaking to the Devil. Analyse how language is used to do this. **3**
3. The final two lines of the poem leave us with a very clear idea of the speaker's own personality. Explain what this is and how this is achieved. **3**
4. Burns's poetry often relates to traditional Scottish life and beliefs. By referring to this and least one other poem, discuss how this is achieved. **10**

Possible answers

1. A delightful picture of Eden is conjured up in stanza 15: 'Sweet on the fragrant flow'ry swaird / In shady bow'r – pleasant word choice backed up by gentle alliteration of 'sw' and 'f' sounds, as well as soothing 'ow' vowels.

   Contrast with stanza 18: repetitive sentence structure 'An how ... /An brak ... / An loused' helps create the sense of the Devil's relentless ill-treatment of his victim, with word choice: 'bizz', 'reekit duds', 'reestit gizz', 'smoutie' – strong sounds and unflattering descriptions showing the Devil at work after the fall from Eden.

   2 marks for a detailed/insightful comment plus a quotation/reference. 1 mark for a more basic comment plus a quotation/reference. 0 marks for a quotation with no comment. Total: 4 marks. (Marks can be gained 2+2, 2+1+1 or 1+1+1+1. For full marks, both sides of the contrast must be covered.)

2. Use of humour, based on directness, cheek, overfamiliarity – to reduce the Devil to level of rascally companion. Plus quotation/reference.

   Disrespectful names and descriptions: 'snick-drawing dog'/ 'auld Cloots' / 'Nickie-ben'. Witty rhyming, for example, 'Ye cam to Paradise incog' (short for incognito).

   Description of the Devil and his activities, making him seem less than awe-inspiring: 'smoutie phiz' [a dirty face] / 'your spiteful joke' refers to the testing of Job through suffering.

   2 marks for a detailed/insightful comment plus a quotation/reference. 1 mark for a more basic comment plus a quotation/reference. 0 marks for a quotation with no comment. Total: 3 marks. (Marks can be gained 2+1 or 1+1+1.)

3. Our sense of him as a carefree, cheerful optimist is strengthened, but then a sensitive sympathetic dimension is suddenly revealed. (**1 mark**)

Strong visual but 'everyday' metaphor for avoiding damnation is his response to the 'black pit' that might await him: 'he'll turn a corner jinkin / An cheat you yet'. Parenthetical 'I dinnae ken' in the final stanza finds him suddenly troubled by the idea of the Devil trapped in hell.

2 marks for a detailed/insightful comment plus a quotation/reference. 1 mark for a more basic comment plus a quotation/reference. 0 marks for a quotation with no comment. Total: 3 marks. (Marks for this part can be gained 2 or 1+1.)

4. **Up to 2 marks for a general explanation of how Burns relates to traditional Scottish life and beliefs (commonality). For example:**

Burns's works are rooted in folk tales, old religious beliefs and superstition and, through his skilful use of narrative style, descriptive power, original angles and humour, he lights up the past/traditional ways for the reader, developing themes which are still relevant.

Up to 2 marks for comments on this section. For example:

We see beliefs about the Devil, for example Bible stories, described with the immediacy of something that has recently happened. Plus quotation/reference.

The Devil seems to be a bit of a trickster who is after your soul but who can be outwitted and for whom we perhaps should feel sorry. This contradicts the general belief in him as supreme evil being. Plus quotation/reference.

3 x 2 marks for comments and references from other poems, of which there are many. Here are just some examples:

- 'Tam o' Shanter' has the everyday traditional setting of a tavern after the market: warm and convivial, with bad weather outside. In this traditional setting, the narrative sees Tam transformed into a mock-heroic character, galloping home, with his heroism (as in traditional stories), undercut by his fear 'glow'ring round with prudent cares' in fear of 'bogles'.
- The view of the Devil in 'Tam o' Shanter' is consistent with 'Address to Deil'. He has turned up in person to pipe for the dancing. There is the combination of ghoulish ('the Dead in their last dresses') with Burns's criticism of extreme Calvinist views ('Twa span-lang, wee, unchristened bairns') doomed to hell despite their innocence.
- In 'Tam o' Shanter' there is a celebration of traditional dancing: 'They reel'd, they set, they cross'd, they cleekit': rhythm and word choice catches the movement of the dance, onward-flowing but with interwoven stops and starts. This seems to express Burns's belief in enjoying life to the full.
- 'To a Mouse': references to seasonal farming activities and life, for example ploughing, harshness of winter used to provide reflection on the human condition.
- 'Holy Willie's Prayer': the intrusive nature of the Kirk into personal lives, *or* the character of Willie – hypocritical and self-serving; challenges the doctrine of 'the Elect'.
- 'A Poet's Welcome to his Love-Begotten Daughter': turns religious/social convention of shame at birth of illegitimate child into pride, *or* shows the huge influence the Kirk had on people's lives.
- 'A Man's a Man for A' That': challenges the accepted divisions in Scottish society which Burns saw around him by stressing the brotherhood of humanity. **Total: 10 marks.**

POETRY
BY LIZ LOCHHEAD

The middle of the twentieth century saw a revival or renaissance of Scottish literature with poetry at its core. Liz Lochhead's first collection, *Memo for Spring*, brought a brilliantly perceptive and lively new voice to this revival. Her poetry was rooted in post-war times of change and presented a freshness of ideas and style. Often referring to her own childhood and her teenage days in the 1960s – and seeing these in the light of the new aspirations and possibilities of the 1970s, 1980s and beyond – Lochhead has produced some of the great poems of modern Scotland. In 2011 she became Scotland's Makar, the official voice of poetry in Scotland and only the second holder of this title. That says it all!

Watch out for her wonderful, often subtle, poetry-crafting as well as for her great ear for colloquial language and her gift for turning the everyday into something special. You will come across these aspects time and again in the six texts you will be studying for your Scottish Text section, and you will also see how skilfully she can conjure up characters and a sense of time and place.

The six Liz Lochhead poems you will study for the Scottish Text section are:

- 'Some Old Photographs'
- 'The Bargain'
- 'View of Scotland/Love Poem'
- 'For my Grandmother Knitting'
- 'My Rival's House'
- 'Last Supper'.

This is a rich and varied selection, dealing with a number of themes such as:

- the relationship between past and present
- love
- the complexity of human relationships
- female attitudes towards men
- what makes life worthwhile.

Poem 1: 'Some Old Photographs'

This poem, published in 2009 but looking back through some photographs and the memories they evoke to the middle of the twentieth century, seems at first nostalgic, though sharply observed and humorous. However, the speaker's determination to see the actual reality of the past strips sentimentality away entirely.

Stanzas 1 and 2

To build up your essential confident knowledge, we will look at some aspects of the opening two stanzas. Here we have the impression of a bundle of photographs – some of 1950s Glasgow scenes, others of family life – being looked through and to some extent discussed by two people, two good friends, perhaps partners. They are Glaswegians themselves. Let's take a closer look:

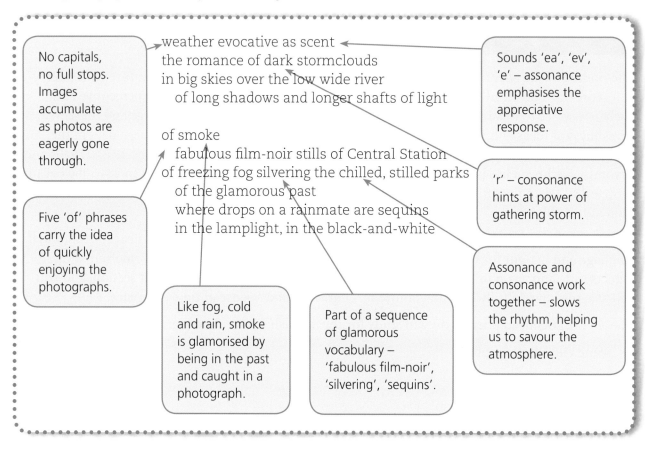

> No capitals, no full stops. Images accumulate as photos are eagerly gone through.

> Five 'of' phrases carry the idea of quickly enjoying the photographs.

> weather evocative as scent
> the romance of dark stormclouds
> in big skies over the low wide river
>   of long shadows and longer shafts of light
>
> of smoke
>   fabulous film-noir stills of Central Station
> of freezing fog silvering the chilled, stilled parks
>   of the glamorous past
>   where drops on a rainmate are sequins
>   in the lamplight, in the black-and-white

> Sounds 'ea', 'ev', 'e' – assonance emphasises the appreciative response.

> 'r' – consonance hints at power of gathering storm.

> Like fog, cold and rain, smoke is glamorised by being in the past and caught in a photograph.

> Part of a sequence of glamorous vocabulary – 'fabulous film-noir', 'silvering', 'sequins'.

> Assonance and consonance work together – slows the rhythm, helping us to savour the atmosphere.

There is no rhyme as such and the rhythm is irregular. You may note how the monosyllabic words of line 3 ('in big skies ... ') help make it a slow, reflective line. Then there are lines 6 and 7 ('fabulous film-noir ... stilled parks'), which seem to tumble along excitedly with their longer words and many repeating, flowing-together sounds. There is certainly a lot of carefully planned poetic language. The vocabulary is fairly familiar, but the more 'glamorous' words help create a magical atmosphere.

It is also important to observe Lochhead's use of sound. This can be assonance as in 'in big skies over the low wide river'. We see the shorter, insignificant vowels of 'in', 'big' and 'river' at start and end, but in the middle we have 'skies ... wide' and 'over ... low', helping to suggest the slow flow of the river and the gaze of those looking at the photo.

Then there is alliteration: 'of long shadows and longer shafts of light'. Here, the limpid quality of the 'l' consonants builds up towards the key word 'light' at the end.

What we have, then, is poetry that effectively conveys the observers' pleasure at what they are seeing and makes us feel it as well.

Stanzas 3 and 4

In stanzas 3 and 4, the photographs seem to move into a more directly personal area, with references to 'your … mother' and the 'Dads'.

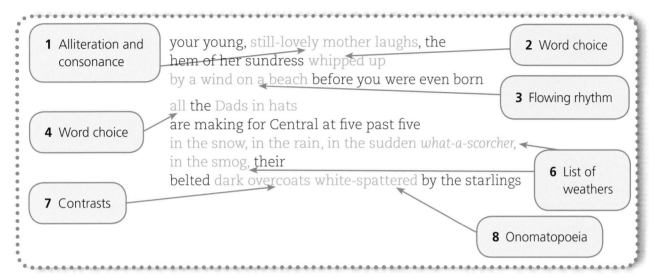

Task

With a partner or in small groups
Read these stanzas carefully, then add your own comments to the boxes provided.

Possible answers

1. Alliteration and consonance: building up towards 'laughs' – helps capture the joyful spontaneity of the mother and the sweetness of the photograph.

2. Word choice: the life and energy of that moment or how the photograph 'immortalises' a split second of the past.

3. Flowing rhythm: this suggests the movement of the wind.

4. Word choice: a time when everything was safely and cosily the same, not chaotic or random.

5. Word choice: familiar, gentle description of nice, affable crowd.

6. List of weathers: makes us think how regular, unchanging the Dads' routine was.

7. Contrasts: help bring out the impact of the starlings on Glasgow citizens in the past.

8. Onomatopoeia: the explosive quality emphasises the physical effect of the starlings.

Stanza 5

Overall, we now have a very positive picture of the past; looking at old photographs can kindle up a warm feeling inside the observer. However, in stanza 5, things change. Watch out for a definite style/context contrast halfway through – and, as a marker, a very short but important word isolated by enjambment at the end of a line:

> This is the first denial of the validity or reality of the photographs.

> above what was
> never really this photograph

> This is the first reference to the photographs in the past tense. Enjambment isolates and emphasises this word.

Enjambment, as you probably know, splits sentences or phrases across line endings where there is not a natural break.

On your own or with a partner

Find three features in stanza 5 that you can analyse in terms of poetical techniques and/or other points of interest in language or content. Here is an example to get you started.

Quote	Analysis
'starlings'	This is the first word in this stanza and the last word in the previous stanza. This keeps a sense of continuity between stanzas and gives the idea of being struck by each photograph but also keen to move on to the next

Questions

Write an answer to this analysis question and, using the ideas discussed on page 90, base your answer on stanza 5, although you might also have to refer to previous stanzas.

Explain how the poet changes the direction of the poem to convey its true theme.

Possible answers

- Previous stanzas are based around flowing, repeating patterns of description '... of ... of ... of' then 'in ... in ... in' – this flow ends on ' ... cloud'.
- The key word 'was' reminds us that the photographs belong to the past and 'never really' denies their portrayal of the reality of the past.
- This is followed immediately by a difficult, odd but very effective phrase: 'but always all the passing now' – insisting the past was no more lovely or orderly than our own 'now'.
- This is illustrated by 'noise and stink and smoky breath' – non-visual reality.
- Use of a metaphor to describe starlings as a 'perfect and permanent cloud', which ends the 'romance' of the past, as starlings in their constant flying and chattering are excellent symbols for change and unruly disorder.
- Word choice: 'perfect' sounds just too good and pushes the observer into reality.

Final stanza

On your own or with a partner

Look again at the final stanza. These three lines counterbalance the rest of the poem: its tone, emotion and message skilfully contradict those of the first four stanzas. You need to know that shipbuilding was once a huge industry on the Clyde and the closure of most of the great shipyards was seen as a disaster for Glasgow.

Try these Scottish Text-type questions.

1. Comment on the length of the final stanza.
2. What feeling about the past does the poem finally express? Think about alliteration and the last line's double meaning.

Possible answers

1. The final stanza's brevity is in contrast to the flowingly descriptive, lyrical quality of the previous descriptions, which it opposes.

   It suggests that the speaker/observer has had enough of old photographs, and whisks her way through the last ones.

2. That the past can seem very seductive, attractive and poignant and a lot more communal and orderly than the present.

   'wee boays ... bunting ... big launch ... boat'. This alliterating list suggests that, in reality, the past is composed of things thrown together for a brief while as time moves along.

   This includes the industry seen in the last photograph: there is a 'boat' about to sail, but this also refers, as a saying, to the shipbuilding industry pictured there, which has since disappeared.

In this poem we have seen Lochhead gazing into the past to elicit truths about how we look for meaning in our lives, and also about how we can kid ourselves. It is a tough vision, and this idea of hers – that we must not linger in the past (although we can value it for what it is worth) – will emerge in other poems.

Poem 2: 'The Bargain'

'... looking back, looking forward': 'The Bargain' is a poem that we can link to 'Some Old Photographs' as it touches on things of the past in order to examine the quality of our lives in the present.

Structure

Structure is important in this subtle personal drama set against the sweeping backdrop of a cold, wet, early January day in Glasgow. It is about what to do with the past and what should be left to the past, explored through the story of an uninspiring visit to Glasgow's Barras Market, although we come to realise that its true topic is a portrait of a relationship at a crossroads, when a decision should be made.

Task

On your own or in small groups

To develop your confident knowledge it is worthwhile looking at how the poem deals with this relationship. Look over the stanza descriptions below and use the grid to fit lettered descriptions to numbered stanzas.

Stanza	1	2	3	4	5	6	7	8	9	10
Description										

A. Suggests that this relationship has become cautious, unexciting and unable to produce unexpected new magic.

B. Captures the carefree nature of being young, confident, adaptable and unhampered by the baggage of the past. (Here, the past is used productively.)

C. At first looking positively about heading off together, until the route becomes difficult – a mistaken choice even.

D. A short stanza about the present puzzle of this relationship.

E. Hopeful, tentatively optimistic – troubled by the feeling that love is not able to transform the world just now.

F. The young couple are intermittently together, sharing viewpoints to some extent, but showing differences in their needs and perspectives.

G. Sums up the present unsatisfactory state of things, comparing this to more clear-cut approaches to life.

H. Takes us into the Barras and then portrays emotional commitment to family life – comparing it to this relationship.

I. Deals with the ongoing attempt to conjure up a sense of shared experience – only partially successful.

J. Suggests that this relationship does not have the commitment of the families with children.

Possible answers

Stanza	1	2	3	4	5	6	7	8	9	10
Description	C	D	B	E	A	H	F	I	G	J

Stanza 8

Now focus on one stanza to see how Lochhead builds up the details and how these relate to her theme.

Task

On your own, with a partner or in small groups

Read stanza 8 again, bearing in mind the theme: how difficult it is to let go (of the past, of a relationship ...). How is the uncertain quality of their love for each other conveyed in this stanza?

Put the following descriptions into the most appropriate boxes in the table below.

1. Similar activities, but these simple actions are symbolically different, showing their separateness.
2. A moment full of physical sensations which should add up to a pleasant experience, but do not quite.
3. Concise, straightforward summary of what is happening, which suggests much more about their relationship.
4. A sense that the couple are cheering no one up and contributing to the dreich atmosphere.
5. We see them being impatient with each other.

Part of stanza 8	Description
'We queue in a blue haze of hot fat for Danny's Do-nuts that grit our teeth with granules of sugar'	
'I keep losing you and finding you –'	
'two stalls away you thumb through a complete set of manuals for primary teachers in the thirties I rub my sleeve on a dusty Chinese saucer till the gilt shows through.'	
'Oh come on we promised we'd not let our affection for the slightly cracked trap us into such expenditure again. Oh even if it is a bargain we won't buy.'	
'The stallholder says I'll be the death of her she says see January It's been the doldrums the day.'	

Possible answers

Part of stanza 8	Description
'We queue in a blue haze of hot fat for Danny's Do-nuts that grit our teeth with granules of sugar'	**2.** A moment full of physical sensations which should add up to a pleasant experience, but do not quite.
'I keep losing you and finding you – '	**3.** Concise, straightforward summary of what is happening, which suggests much more about their relationship.
'two stalls away you thumb through a complete set of manuals for primary teachers in the thirties I rub my sleeve on a dusty Chinese saucer till the gilt shows through.'	**1.** Similar activities, but these simple actions are symbolically different, showing their separateness.
'Oh come on we promised we'd not let our affection for the slightly cracked trap us into such expenditure again. Oh even if it is a bargain we won't buy.'	**5.** We see them being impatient with each other.
'The stallholder says I'll be the death of her she says see January It's been the doldrums the day.'	**4.** A sense that the couple are cheering no one up and contributing to the dreich atmosphere.

And think about this before moving on – at times they are still a couple, but one recurring aspect of the poem is that of separation, of going in different directions. Try to find more examples of groups of two, or of two different perspectives. (Think about the month and football supporters.)

On your own/with a partner

Building your analysis skills

Try these analysis questions based on stanza 8.

1. How does Lochhead use language to evoke a certain mood at the start of the stanza?
2. How is a sense of 'love under pressure' conveyed?
3. Show how Lochhead builds up to the concluding line through the second half of the stanza. ('Doldrums' means the misery brought on by doing nothing and getting nowhere. This term once applied to sailing ships when the wind had died away.)

Possible answers

1. Despite the warmth of the stall on a cold day, it seems claustrophobically smoky and unpleasant.

    The line endings of 'fat', 'grit', 'sugar' help suggest unhealthy discomfort.

    Alliteration and assonance in the short words of the first line back up the feeling of being trapped in the queue; or unpleasant texture: onomatopoeia/alliteration of 'grit ... granules'.

2. The short line 'I keep' suggests trying hard and not being relaxed.

    'losing you and finding you –' emphasises constant stressed alertness; or neither harmonising together nor relaxed when apart.

    He is looking at vaguely instructive, practical things; she is seeking out beauty; or rubbing at the saucer symbolises the work she is putting into the relationship. (Make up your own mind about guilt/gilt pun.)

3. The repetition of 'Oh' suggests a tone of impatience.

  'we promised / we'd not let', 'we won't buy' – all joint statements looking back or negative, never spontaneous or pointing ahead.

  'a' assonance leads from 'affection' through 'cracked' to 'trap' – a very negative word at the start of the line.

  'expenditure' word choice: a stuffy, formal, joyless word.

  The short declarative line 'we won't buy' is again very negative.

Task

On your own or with a partner
Find three things that help create a sense of place.

Possible answers

- References to the river 'fast and high', 'big quick', 'the dark coming early and as cold as the river', at or near the start and near the end of the poem, suggest excitement of the city at first, although finally its presence is gloomy.
- The portrayal of the squalor of Paddy's Market – focusing on smell and one particular man.
- The portrayal of the liveliness and variety of the Barras – a realistic sense that most things purchased are useless.

Try making 'sense of place' links between 'The Bargain' and 'Some Old Photographs' before moving on to the next poem.

Poem 3: 'View of Scotland/Love Poem'

The past is not always a drag-anchor on the present, but it can be something to value and contrast with our own lives – especially when it involves family and the personal past from which we have moved on. In 'View of Scotland/Love Poem', Lochhead examines the past and considers what really matters in life. As you study this text, keep thinking of connections with the previous poems.

With its dual title, which can be applied to the first and second halves of the poem, this piece forms a double-take on 31 December. First comes a memory of every childhood Hogmanay ('too ordinary to be nostalgia'); then, with a blink, we are into the present 30 years on, the speaker talking to her partner as the old year nears its end. By considering the two halves, we can observe how the second half balances, develops and contrasts with the first half.

Stanzas 1 and 2
The first two stanzas are a bittersweet but intentionally non-nostalgic view of the speaker's mother preparing for the arrival of the New Year. Character creation is a great gift of Lochhead. What impression do we gain of 'my mother' as a character?

Task

In small groups

Here is a list of the mother's attributes from stanza 1. Find a quotation of any length from the stanza which provides evidence for each attribute.

Mother's attribute	Quotation
Obsessively and energetically house-proud	
Has a conventional 1950s view of what is classy, special food	
Is more influenced by ritual than reality	
Likes things done neatly	
Uses clichés rather than depressing truths	

Possible answers

Mother's attribute	Quotation
Obsessively and energetically house-proud	*'Down on her hands and knees / at ten at night on Hogmanay'*
Has a conventional 1950s view of what is classy, special food	*'a newly opened tin of sockeye salmon'*
Is more influenced by ritual than reality	*'Though we do not expect anyone'*
Likes things done neatly	*'petticoat-tails fanned out'*
Uses clichés rather than depressing truths	*'"Last year it was very quiet"'*

This is a picture is of a 1950s mother 'getting it right' within the conventions of Hogmanay. The poem shows us determined commitment, then 'tasteful' hospitality, while twice pointing out the futility of the preparations.

With a partner or in small groups

Look at stanza 2. Find quotations of any length to match the following technique descriptions. Where you can, comment on how the quotation backs up the technique description.

Technique description	Quotation	Comment
A physical description based on details of the 1950s		
A line featuring internal rhyme to show just how proudly neat mother is (think of two short rhyming lines turned into one)		
A line containing a visual image of something laid out and waiting		
A line that uses colloquial language to show us mother urging herself on		

Technique description	Quotation	Comment
Three lines that use a clutter of monosyllabic words to slow the rhythm, helping to fix their important message in our minds		
An ironic line in the context that mother will not change her routines from year to year in her little bit of Scotland		
A symbolic suggestion that new and old are easily interchangeable		

Possible answers

Technique description	Quotation	Comment
A physical description based on details of the 1950s	'Mum's got her rollers in with waveset'	Mother's hair will only be released when the work is done – just before the Bells
A line featuring internal rhyme to show just how proudly neat mother is (think of two short rhyming lines turned into one)	'and her well-pressed good dress'	The four strong stresses in 'well-pressed good dress' emphasise the internal rhyme, conveying idea of controlled, conscious effort to look her best
A line containing a visual image of something laid out and waiting	'slack across the candlewick upstairs'	'Candlewick' is another period detail. The one good dress lying waiting seems quite poignant
A line that uses colloquial language to show us mother urging herself on	'Nearly half-ten already and her not shifted!'	Note the exclamation mark
Three lines that use a clutter of monosyllabic words to slow the rhythm, helping to fix their important message in our minds	'If we're even to hope to prosper / this midnight must find us / how we would like to be'	Quite superstitious – 'we' and 'us' tell us it's a shared belief
An ironic line in the context that mother will not change her routines from year to year in her little bit of Scotland	'A new view of Scotland'	One picture of the bens and glens must last all year
A symbolic suggestion that new and old are easily interchangeable	'with a dangling calendar / is propped under last year's, / ready to take its place'	No great change is expected year by year

Questions

Try this analysis question, based on stanzas 1 and 2.

Analyse how Lochhead uses language to convey the importance of preparing the house correctly.

Possible answers

- All-out physical effort by the mother is expressed in energetic colloquial phrases such as 'giving it elbow grease / jiffywaxing the vinolay' and her exclamation that she's still 'not shifted!'
- The attempt to make 'the slab of black bun' seem delicate and genteel: 'petticoat-tails fanned out / on bone china' – choice of traditional 'feminine' words (petticoat and fanned) and reference to the special-occasion 'bone china'.
- Naive but genuine statement of superstition: 'this midnight must find us / how we would like to be' – monosyllables slow down the rhythm among all the hectic preparations.

Stanzas 3 and 4

Now turn to the second half of the poem (stanzas 3 and 4). A fruitful way to tackle this is through noting some differences to the first half (stanzas 1 and 2).

On your own or with a partner

Try to find a contrast between the first and second halves of the poem for each description provided. The first one has been done for you.

First half	Second half
'Hogmanay' – traditionally special	'December thirty-first' – an ordinary day
	Speaking directly to partner/lover
Childhood memories	
	New Year now very personal and truly happy
Refers only to her own family	
Waiting for 'the Bells' is all-important	
	Sense of time passing – so make the most of it

The theme that emerges is one of moving from a ritual to something more rich, meaningful and personal.

On your own or with a partner

1. Stanza 3 is one sentence long. How does this compare with the sentences in stanzas 1 and 2?
2. (a) How often is the word 'we' used in stanza 3?
   (b) In which half are all these examples found?
3. What is the effect of the stanza's opening word?
4. What is the effect of the stanza's final two words?

Using the ideas in the answers to questions 1 to 4, tackle question 5.

5. Explain the transforming impact stanza 3 has on the poem.

Possible answers

1. It is much longer, more continuous and flowing.

2. (a) Four.
   (b) All in the second half, which creates a more personal tone.

3. The word 'Darling' immediately identifies the person being spoken to and suggests strong, confident affection. It changes the focus of the poem from childhood past to very personal present.

4. The use of 'did we?' confirms the affectionate tone of 'Darling'. It is a rhetorical question with no doubt about the answer.

5. Stanza 3 creates a different, more intimate and personal tone through the opening 'Darling' and proliferation of 'we's, finishing with a relaxed rhetorical question, 'did we?'

   It begins in the present tense but distances present from past: 'thirty years since'.

   The long involved sentence is not like the collection of memories seen earlier, but it is a mature statement about the life they have chosen.

   The second half of the sentence is a beautiful evocation of love (which repeated we's, 'w' alliteration and 'when/Bells/went' assonance emphasise).

Questions

Looking at the last stanza, read from '... their best spread of plenty'. It is the balancing point of the final stanza: beforehand we see the city readying itself for the New Year, and this phrase sums it up. Now tackle these analysis questions.

1. Analyse the effect of the phrase 'their best spread of plenty'.
2. The lines '(for to even hope to prosper / this midnight must find us / how we would like to be)' appear in this stanza and earlier in the poem. Explain the contrast between their two meanings.
3. Comment on the New Year supplies this couple has chosen.
4. The poem concludes on a note of romantic togetherness. Analyse how this is achieved.

Possible answers

1. The phrase suggests a welcoming generosity of spirit emphasised by the assonance of the four key words.

2. In stanza 2, it justified a hectic ritual: here it seems truly part of the richness of celebration, part of a joint decision to enjoy the New Year.

3. 'sickly liqueur' because it is unappetising, obviously not for them, but for an expected visitor/link to the past.

   '... steak pies / like quilts on a double bed' – a comforting simile that suggests the warmth of their relationship.

4. 'And this is where we live. / There is no time like the / present for a kiss.' The first sentence restates, with brilliant simplicity, that sense of confident togetherness.

   The second sentence shows why Hogmanay is so good for them – they do not need it. They do not need to wait for the Bells because the present moment is happy in itself. The enjambment of 'the present' highlights 'present' at start of the last line. Delicate sound echoes (assonance, consonance) lead up to their personal 'kiss': 'this is ... live. There is ... kiss'.

Now you're aware of the celebratory nature of some of Lochhead's work. The next poem combines celebration of life with a poignant sense of its fleeting nature.

Poem 4: 'For my Grandmother Knitting'

This poem contains many of the elements seen in Lochhead's work so far:

- It offers an exploration of the past: a tough past, but one in which Grandmother was definitely at home.

- It observes Grandmother's hands: arthritic and painful, but still able and willing to knit ceaselessly.

- It is unrhymed and irregular in lines, rhythm and stanzas, but as full of patterns as a knitting magazine!

Structure

It is with this idea of patterns – or Lochhead's structural framework – that the study of this touching, empathetic poem begins.

Stanzas 1 to 3 take us into Grandmother's past where we see her ever-busy hands at work, making life happen. In stanza 4 the poem switches to the present and a generic Sunday visit that emphasises the loss of continuity between Grandmother's knitting skills and the family's needs.

On your own, with a partner or in small groups

Look for examples of repetition of key words and phrases, both within individual stanzas and throughout the poem. This will help identify the patterns that help to shape this poem. You have been given some examples to start you off.

Stanza	Examples of repetition
1	'no need' 'hands' x 3
2	
3	
4	'no need'
5	

Possible answers

Stanza	Examples of repetition
1	'hands' x 3 'no need' 'they say' 'in the working of your hands' 'easily' 'as if your hands'

Stanza	Examples of repetition
2	'necessity'
3	'hands' x 5 'they say' 'no need' 'in the working of your hands' 'once the hands' x 3 'necessary'
4	'they say' x 2 'no need' 'too much' x 2 'necessity'
5	'hands' x 4 'in the working of your hands' 'easily' 'as if your hands' x 2

Points to note:

- The word 'hands' appears 12 times in the poem, emphasising what is still making life meaningful for Grandmother.

- Stanzas 1 and 5 are very similar. As opening and closing stanzas, these frame the poem and give it an overarching structure.

- Stanza 1 begins with well-meant but negative family advice. Otherwise it deals positively with knitting skill and links it to the past: 'as if your hands / were once again those sure and skilful hands / of the fisher-girl'.

- The rhythm moves along very lightly from '... the needles still move' (contradicting 'no need', which 'needles' echoes). This would seem to capture the easy flow of Grandmother's knitting.

Task

On your own or with a partner

Stanzas 1 and 5 are similar in several ways, but the tone of stanza 5 is much more poignant. List the key features that bring about this change of tone.

Possible answers

- Farewell after a visit, focusing on Grandmother's goodbye wave – with her hands for once seen separate from her knitting needles.
- For the first time we see how her precious, wonderful hands look now – the first actual description of them. The rhythm is slow because of the one-word, full-stopped, minor sentences.
- The final descriptive word 'Old' in line 5 emphasises that they will not get better.
- The miracle that the hands still move and knit so well is tinged with sadness now, but see how the easy 'knitting rhythm' starts up after the emphatic full stops of line 5 had slowed things down.
- The 'as if' clauses now more striking – in stanza 1, she was compared to the girl she once was but now we are made aware that knitting is the only thing keeping her going.

Stanzas 2 and 3

In stanza 2 'deft and swift' leads into the richly onomatopoeic 'You slit the still-ticking quick silver fish'. This captures the skill and difficulty of fish-gutting and prepares us for stanza 3's 'biography' of Grandmother's busy hands.

Looking at stanzas 2 and 3, tackle these analysis questions.

1. For the second time, in stanza 3 'no need' and 'needles move' are found close together. Explain why.
2. What does the repetition of 'once the hands of ...' add to the rhythm of stanza 3?
3. What overall picture of Grandmother's life do we get here?
4. Analyse the last six lines of stanza 3 to show how Lochhead's use of language:
   (a) conveys the toughness of Grandmother's life at that time
   (b) puts over a sense of her coping despite the difficulties.

Possible answers

1. These phrases help to emphasise the contrast between what she does for the family and what the family is telling her.

2. The rhythm captures the repetitive action of knitting. It gives the impression of Grandmother knitting her way through all the phases of her life.

3. A busy, practical, hands-on sort of life where she had to turn her hand to many things.

4. (a) There is a list of activities, all of which involve effort or hardship – emphasised by alliteration.
   (b) 'made do and mended' and 'scraped and slaved' are paired expressions with alliteration, assonance and consonance, which suggests some sort of organisation despite difficulty – as does the final short line 'when necessary'.

On your own, with a partner or in small groups

What other links could you make with Lochhead poems you have studied so far? The list below gives three themes that might come up in that final 10-mark question in the Scottish Text Question paper. Using each theme, work out links between 'For my Grandmother Knitting' and other poems you have studied.

- The past.
- Celebration.
- What we should really value in life.

Possible answers

The past
- This poem is enriched by references to Grandmother's past.
- Links to 'Some Old Photographs' and 'View of Scotland/Love Poem'.

Celebration
- Celebration of Grandmother's endurance through difficult times and poverty, and of her enduring skill.
- Links to 'Some Old Photographs' (where the 'celebration' is finally undermined) and the second half of 'View of Scotland/Love Poem'.

What we should really value in life
- Pinpoints Grandmother's skills and the quality of life that knitting things for the family brings her.
- All the other poems focus on the importance of warmth and love over observing the rituals, and show material possessions (however much a 'bargain') are meaningless without that warmth and love. 'Some Old Photographs' turns it around by suggesting what should *not* be valued.

Poem 5: 'My Rival's House'

This poem is different from what we have studied so far – and yet, like 'For my Grandmother Knitting', it is a masterly piece of character creation, if not in this case an appreciative, affectionate one.

Its narrative is the first visit by the speaker, young and female, to the family home of her boyfriend, where, as the 'Lady of the house / Queen bee', his mother presides. We can also see a theme of entrenched and powerful traditional woman (the mother is apparently middle-class and wealthy) exerting what we would now call her passive-aggressive, matriarchal influence over her world. The new, emerging woman, seeking a true control over her own life, and honest rather than manipulative partnership, is an enemy. In the more basic terms of son, mother and girlfriend, the mother simply does not want to let go.

Stanzas 1 and 2

These stanzas show us the house itself. The house expresses, symbolically, the spirit of the person who has decorated it – the 'rival' (mother).

> Ormolu is a gold-coloured covering for intricate metalwork. Gilt is usually thin gold leaf, and satin is plain on one side, shiny and silky on the other.

On your own, with a partner or in small groups

These multiple-choice questions allow you to examine this symbolism and some aspects of Lochhead's language skills.

Stanza 1

1. Does 'peopled' suggest that this house is:
   A. busy and bustling with life
   B. a place where lots of decorations and furniture have replaced people?
2. 'surfaces' suggests:
   A. something beautiful and alluring
   B. something a bit inhuman and off-putting
3. Which line develops the idea of 'surfaces'?
   A. line 2
   B. line 3
4. Which word in line 4 seems to sum up the theme?
   A. 'stiff'
   B. 'sink'
5. The slightly faster rhythm of line 5 helps:
   A. to bring out a more relaxed feeling
   B. to suggest a kind of gathering paranoia

Stanza 2

6. The enjambments of the second stanza:
   A. help to suggest the speaker's admiration for this beautiful place
   B. underline the mother's obsessively tidy attitude
7. The fact that the lines rhyme:
   A. adds a jollier, brighter tone to the poem
   B. makes everything appear all the more controlled and restricted
8. The rhythm is:
   A. very regular, suggesting the orderliness of the house
   B. variable, stop-start, suggesting the edgy nervousness of the speaker
9. Finally, comment on the first two lines of stanza 2, showing what they suggest about the effect of the house and the mother on the speaker and how they do so.

Possible answers

1. B – seems to emphasise the lack of life. It is the mother's domain, kept perfect and free from messy people.

2. B – suggests a lack of depth, a superficiality.

3. A – all these things produce a surface sheen only – what is beneath is different. Ormolu sounds ornate and fussy/expensive. The couches seem welcoming at first.

4. A – '... couches, / cushions so stiff' – these should be comfortable and 'cosy', but in fact are the opposite.

5. B – 'distortions' is what stretches the line out and it is this which suggests a nightmare quality.

6. B – 'parquet floor' takes on a significance which 'must' emphasises and, of course, 'Dust' is the great enemy of the house-proud mother.

7. A – Lochhead is a brilliant rhymester, but is very sparing of it in her serious verse. Its purpose here is to strengthen the theme of alienation.

8. B – longer/shorter lines, enjambment, a flowing line juxtaposed to a broken-up one – these all contribute to the variable rhythm.

9. Word choice of 'her door', 'shuffle', 'tiptoe' and the line break after 'tiptoe', the sense of being oddly 'stocking-soled' at her behest – these all help create a sense of the speaker feeling uncertain, confused and unpleasantly controlled.

Stanza 3

This stanza begins with more ornamentation, 'silver' this time, but rapidly becomes personal as the battle lines are drawn. A look at Lochhead's use of rhythm here will help to demonstrate the way that their surface behaviour – taking tea together politely – is barely able to conceal what is really going on.

Task

On your own, with a partner or in small groups

Create two lists. The first list should include lines from stanza 3, either singly or a few together, which seem to flow smoothly at an even pace or which seem balanced and orderly. The other list should feature lines or short sections that seem at odds with this even flow.

Flowing rhythm	Disrupted rhythm

Possible answers

Flowing rhythm	Disrupted rhythm
Lines 1 to 3: 'Silver … him and me'. Alliteration and consonance really help to smooth this along: silver, sugar, salver, rival, serves, glosses	Line 4: quick descent into awkward self-conscious loss of confidence signalled by word choice and stop/start rhythm
Line 5 – '… and yet my rival thinks she means me well' – a very regular line indeed	Line 6: from the unpleasant, animal-like 'squirms' onwards (contradicting the mother's surface properness), it seems to pick up a kind of panicky quality. The previous line was a most regular ten-syllable line (an iambic pentameter). This line has just one extra syllable, but that is enough to disrupt the rhythm despite the rhyme
Lines 10 and 11: line 10 may seem more chopped up, but longer polysyllabic words tend to flow and alliteration/consonance ('d' and 'r'/'l') help here	Lines 7 to 9: there are little balances within these two lines, but the widely varying line lengths and the 'fight, fight' repetition break things up

What is the impact of this on stanza 3 and the development of the poem? Let's see how rhythm ties in with other aspects. The stanza has a smooth, 'polite' start, until the word 'glosses' indicates the mother's disdain. It is a 'surface' word, a thin coat of paint or a mild passing interest – the mother has little concern for 'him and me' as a pairing.

Then the rhythm breaks up: 'I am all edges, a surface, a shell': three metaphors that ironically echo the furnishings of the house as they show us the speaker's state of mind. The following, rhyming, line – very smooth and regular – shows the patronising composure of the mother: 'and yet my rival thinks she means me well'.

The next line, still part of this section of '-ell' rhymes, is the turning point of the stanza, revealing what the speaker knows is coming; 'squirms' suggests something animal-like, eager to be out in the open. Notice how Lochhead takes the old, now clichéd saying of 'fighting tooth and nail' and customises it for her needs here. The vicious determination of the cliché is only diminished slightly in 'capped tooth, polished nail', suggesting a veneer of civilisation, and then intensified with the alliteration and broken rhythm of 'fight, fight foul'.

The final two lines seem more sedate, but now we know fully how the speaker is suffering as she maintains this respectful role. This is brilliant writing, bristling with restrained tension. The unexpected half-rhyme of 'sip' and 'cup' does enough in itself to provide a sense of disharmony, but 'bitter' leaves us in no doubt that she hates being there in the power of this woman.

Stanzas 4 to 6

In the final three stanzas we are given glimpses of the mother's manipulative combat methods, and Lochhead uses metaphor to convey some aspects of these. Metaphors have not been prevalent in the selection so far, but she is as adept with these as with all other techniques.

Task

On your own, with a partner or in small groups

Select two of Lochhead's metaphors from stanzas 4 to 6, and in turn, quote and comment fully on them.

Possible answers

- 'This son she bore – / first blood to her' – he was her first born or his 'first blood' came from her (which explains the speaker's thankfulness). But, metaphorically, as they now begin to fight for the (almost anonymous) young man, the mother lands first blow and has first advantage. She gave birth to him!
- 'never, never can escape scot free' – a sense that his personality has been, at least partially, shaped by his family (that is, his mother). There is no escape from that influence.
- 'the sour potluck of family' – links to 'bitter cup' and takes the cliché of 'potluck' back to its cooking origins. You cannot choose your family background and this unfortunate family 'pot' contains something very 'sour', a malevolent, possessive, jealous streak. Will it affect him also?
- 'oh how close' – the 'close' family is another cliché and is usually meant positively. Here it takes on a kind of claustrophobic, smothering, threatening sense.
- 'the family that furnishes my rival's place' – are there lots of photographs of high-achieving, much-loved, family members, all superior to this new girlfriend, around the place? Is it simply the wealth that has been bestowed on this house by a successful family? Whatever, it is intimidating.
- 'Queen bee' – only one queen per hive is probably the most potent point of comparison and any young rival is killed. It is an interesting development of the idea that, like an insect, she is just doing what she must do and that is why the speaker struggles to match her: 'She is far more unconscious / far more dangerous than me'.
- 'dreams for breakfast. / Dinner, and her salt tears pepper our soup' – these two mealtime metaphors suggest that the mother is taking every opportunity to impose her vision of her boy's future on the visitors by using her full emotional range and controlling through emotion.

Task

On your own, with a partner or in small groups

So, which topics arise from this poem and with which other poems can comparisons be made? Here is a short list of features that might arise in 10-mark Scottish text questions. They all relate to 'My Rival's House'. Which of the other poems so far could these features also relate to?

A. Portrayal of character.
B. Obsessiveness.
C. Insight into emotions of speaker.
D. Our negative side.
E. The influence of family.
F. The power of poetic techniques.
G. Creating atmosphere.

Possible answers

'Some Old Photographs': F and G.

'The Bargain': C, F and G.

'View of Scotland/Love Poem': B, D, F and G.

'For my Grandmother Knitting': A, B, C and F.

Poem 6: 'Last Supper'

One love of Lochhead's is to transform well-known old stories in her poetry. These can be family tales, legends, traditional literature or Bible stories. When mixed with her wonderful observation and her witty, ironic use of modern clichés, something quite unique emerges. This is what we find in 'Last Supper', which also blends in puns, startling metaphors and attitude!

A woman – not, this time, the speaker – prepares for a final meal with her boyfriend before parting from him. She goes on to imagine sharing the story of this event with two female friends. Lochhead brings two differing perceptions to this poem. She is not prepared to dish out simple answers. On the one hand there is the female/feminist mockery of male 'objectifying' of women. This discarded boyfriend becomes a metaphorical meal for the friends. On the other hand the women are not portrayed at all sympathetically, so there is a double criticism going on. Is Lochhead simply looking for a balance, deploring the stupidity of the sexual warfare that pits male dishonesty against the 'savage integrity' of women when they close ranks?

Task

On your own

There are several cultural references in this poem. Carry out some background research on the internet for each of the following:

- The Bible's Last Supper: Christ has what will be his last meal with his disciples and identifies Judas as the one who will betray him.
- Shakespeare's *Macbeth*: Macbeth is led astray by three witches who, unknown to him, are plotting his downfall. He is also willing to abandon loyalty and honesty to gain what he wants.
- 'The Twa Corbies': in this ancient ballad, two ravens gleefully prepare to devour the body of a dead knight who has been abandoned by his 'lady fair'.

There are many references to betrayal and death!

Stanza 1

On your own or with a partner

This stanza appears to show the main character poised and ready to strike: to end the relationship with her betraying lover in a clinical way.

Write down any words, phrases, lines or short sections that provide this sense of composed control. Where you can, comment on how the technique backs up the quotation. You should consider the use of common sayings, understatement, word choice, metaphor, enjambment and alliteration. One example has been completed to start you off.

Quote	Technique	Comment
'getting good and ready to renounce'	Alliteration/assonance. Common saying – *'good and ready'*	Techniques emphasise a no-nonsense approach

Possible answers

Quote	Technique	Comment
'getting good and ready to renounce'	Alliteration/assonance. Common saying – *'good and ready'*	Techniques emphasise a no-nonsense approach
'his sweet flesh'	Religious metaphor	Giving up sex with her lover compared to Lenten sacrifice
'(For / Ever)'	Parenthesis/capitals/cliché	Emphasises a definite decision
'assembling the ingredients'	Metaphor	Comparison to a business-like process
'tearing foliage'	Word choice – *'tearing'*	Suggests strength of purpose
'nicely al- / dente vegetables'	Enjambment	Suggests control or savouring her revenge – pausing before the bite

The stanza's superb last two lines need a special note. They contain a paradox: the idea of depending on someone for betrayal seems at first illogical and needs some thought to make sense. They also contain zeugma (one verb relating to two different objects, one ordinary and the other significant). 'the bottle' and 'betrayal with a kiss' are combined together (through 'bring'), surprisingly, as the two things he brings are so different: one very mundane (the bottle), the other very crucial (betrayal), although this is the understated, 'added-on' one. There is also Judas's betrayal of Christ with a kiss, and alliteration and consonance in there to tie the meaning together.

Stanzas 2 and 3

The thing missing in this poem is the meal itself: her thoughts go immediately beyond it. The faithless male lover is never present and the poem now focuses on thoughts of afterwards.

Here there seems a less sure sense of control as food becomes even more of a metaphor: her discussion with 'The Girls' will be the 'leftover hash' of the event, 'extra / tasty if not elegant' – in other words, a bit of a mess. The three friends are caught in a paraphrased line from *Macbeth* when those three 'met again', which refers to the malicious witches.

In stanza 3, the 'cackling around the cauldron' refers to three friends empathising as they dissect a potentially upsetting situation, but Lochhead picks apart this conversation very critically.

In the first half they are discrediting the lover in any way possible.

Task

With a partner or in small groups

1. What impression of 'The Girls' do we derive from the description 'cackling around the cauldron'?
2. The first nine lines of stanza 3 are an extended metaphor: deploring the lover's behaviour and his personality is seen as a meal which they can all richly enjoy. Take one item from this meal, then comment on what it might mean and how this meaning is put across.
3. The second half of stanza 3 brings in a new extended metaphor while maintaining the food one. This is based on 'The Twa Corbies' (check back for elucidation).
   (a) Make a list of the key words and phrases relating to the 'The Girls' here.
   (b) Write a brief commentary on what judgement this metaphor and this word choice lead us to make about them.
   (c) Briefly note down what effect this judgement has on the overall effect, message or theme of the poem.

Possible answers

1. Not very favourable – Lochhead does not dispute Shakespeare's view of witches as destructive and delighted to see destruction, although, of course, in this case it was justified destruction.

2. 'spitting out the gristlier bits / of his giblets' – giblets are the inner organs and spitting suggests a fairly contemptuous dismissal of him once they have fully enjoyed revelations about his secrets. Lochhead uses assonance and consonance for emphasis.

3. (a) gorged/savage integrity/sleek/preening/bright eyes/satisfied
   (b) Female bonding, of course – but there is something pitiless, uncivilised and eventually self-satisfied about the friends.
   (c) The male lover is the villain of the piece, but he has been thoroughly backgrounded: the poem is all about female dignity, humanity and self-respect – the realisation that it is not good for your inner being to become predatory or vindictive, woman or not.

Using your knowledge of all the poems

Scottish Text questions

Look again at 'View of Scotland/Love Poem', then tackle these analysis questions. The final question asks you to link 'View of Scotland/Love Poem' to the other poems.

1.	Liz Lochhead creates a vivid impression of the mother in stanza 1. By referring to both ideas and language, discuss how she does this.	3
2.	How does Lochhead convey the importance of New Year rituals in stanza 2?	2
3.	There is a powerful sense of a loving relationship in stanza 3. Analyse how Lochhead uses language to convey this.	2
4.	Explain why the last three lines are a successful conclusion to the poem.	3
5.	By referring to this and at least one other poem by Lochhead, discuss how she uses contrast in her work.	10

Possible answers

1. Obsessively hard-working/obsessively concerned about New Year preparations.

   Physical description of sheer effort/symbolic of worship as poem opens, emphasised by lateness: 'at ten at night'.

   Energetic word choice: 'giving it elbowgrease' or 'jiffywaxing the vinolay'.

   Use of present participles 'giving'/'jiffywaxing': job ongoing and not finished quickly.

   Parenthesis stating this level of commitment was not unusual.

   Uncomplaining/fatalistic/accepting sort of person: her euphemism ('*Last year it was very quiet ...*') tells us no one came, but she soldiers on this year all the same. The ellipsis after 'quiet' suggests her unspoken sadness about this.

   2 marks for a detailed/insightful comment plus a quotation/reference. 1 mark for a more basic comment plus a quotation/reference. 0 marks for a quotation with no comment. Total: 3 marks. (Marks can be gained 2+1 or 1+1+1.)

2. The mother's implied urging (to herself) to get the preparation done: 'her not shifted!' suggests the need to do this right (**1 mark**).

   The new calendar 'propped' and 'ready': word choice suggests that everything is geared up to the moment the year changes (**1 mark**). **Total: 2 marks.**

3. Word choice: 'Darling' immediately creates the warm tone that is emphasised in last three lines by use of 'we' four times.

   Sentence structure: long, flowing sentence moves through time to focus on their two years together and reach a climax with the very relaxed, confident rhetorical question.

   2 marks for a detailed/insightful comment plus a quotation/reference. 1 mark for a more basic comment plus a quotation/reference. 0 marks for a quotation with no comment. Total: 2 marks. (Marks can be gained 2 or 1+1.)

4. They emphasise the very personal theme of love, giving true meaning to Hogmanay, which has emerged in the poem's second half.

   A very simple statement of what makes home really special: not ceremonies but sharing it.

The idea of celebrating the 'now', the 'present' with a kiss, rather than waiting for the public moment of the Bells – emphasised by 'kiss' as the final word.

2 marks for a detailed/insightful comment plus a quotation/reference; 1 mark for a more basic comment plus a quotation/reference. 0 marks for a quotation with no comment. Total: 3 marks. (Marks can be gained 2+1 or 1+1+1.)

5. **Up to 2 marks for a general explanation of how contrast is used in Lochhead's poetry (commonality). For example:**

Lochhead is adept at using contrast to illuminate theme, often when considering how the past and present impact on people and places. Her keen observation and ability to create atmosphere help her to use contrast effectively.

Up to 2 marks for comments on this section. For example:

Past Hogmanays, where huge and largely futile efforts were made by the mother to observe the 'public' rituals, versus the present Hogmanay, with the intimacy of the couple celebrating for themselves.

3 x 2 marks for comments and references from other poems, of which there are many. Here are some examples:

- 'For my Grandmother Knitting': past and present contrast – Grandmother constantly working in the past, to support her family, versus the present, when only her knitting seems to sustain her and her family do not need or value her efforts.
- 'Some Old Photographs': the past is shown in a sequence of photographs to portray its glamour versus the criticism of false portrayal of the past, which was no less messy or confusing than the present.
- 'My Rival's House': the surface of politeness and civilisation versus the fierce battle going on for the rival's son.
- 'Last Supper': contrast between pain of 'betrayal' and the fierce enjoyment of the 'Girls' when digesting the story of the parting. **Total: 10 marks.**

CRITICAL ESSAY

In your Higher exam you will write **one** critical essay. This can be on drama, prose (fiction or non-fiction), poetry, film/television or language. Most people choose to write about drama, prose fiction or poetry: the three genres you will also study for your Scottish Text section.

Remember

- You *must not* choose the same genre for both the Scottish Text section and the Critical Essay.
- You should aim to spend 45 minutes on the Scottish Text questions and 45 minutes on your essay. The total Critical Reading exam time is 1 hour 30 minutes.
- The Scottish Text section comes first in the exam paper. You might want to get it out of the way first, before choosing your essay. However, you do not have to. You can write the essay first, if you prefer.

A successful essay performance starts with choosing the best question. Here are some tips for making that vital choice:

- There are three questions in each genre section. Remember you choose only one out of all the questions in the Critical Essay section.

- The questions are designed to be 'text friendly'. The SQA does not want to catch you out with questions that fit only obscure titles. The aim is that, across any genre section of three questions, there should be something for everyone.

- That does not mean that every single question will fit every text: that would be impossible. However, across the three questions in each genre, there should be something you can write about.

- Careful choosing is important. This is your one chance to show the SQA what you can do as an essay writer, so make sure you choose the question that allows you to show your knowledge and skills best.

- Make sure you read through all the questions in the section before you make your choice. Also make sure you read the whole question, not just the first few words. Each question will be worded clearly: again, the SQA is not trying to catch you out.

- If you have studied one text from the Scottish text list and one (or more than one) other text, then use your other text (or one of them) for the critical essay.

- If you have studied more than one text from the Scottish text list, you can write your critical essay on one of these. You should write your essay on a Scottish list text *only* if you have another one from the list for your Scottish Text questions. Do not use up your only Scottish list text on the essay: you will need it for the Scottish Text section.

What does the SQA look for in a critical essay?

The examiner marking your essay will be an experienced English teacher and will have clear guidelines to follow. He or she will mark your essay holistically (meaning that they will consider the whole thing, not broken into separate segments), looking for the following points:

- knowledge and understanding

- analysis of the text

- evaluation

- technical accuracy

- relevance to the question.

Throughout the year you will practise your essay planning and writing skills. There are various ways you can do this, including:

- spider diagrams

- paragraph plans, bullet-pointing your main ideas

- matching quotations to points you wish to make

- practising writing introductions quickly

- creating topic sentences to start off your paragraphs

- in groups, writing a paragraph each of an essay you have planned

- making up essay questions on your text(s) and swapping them with other students, then giving them feedback on their efforts

- writing practice essays individually.

Some people have a particular acronym they use to help them structure essays, such as a checklist of things they need to include in each paragraph. For example:

P make a POINT

E provide EVIDENCE (this might be a quotation)

E EVALUATION

L LINK with the next paragraph

or

S STATEMENT – the main point you wish to make

Q QUOTATION or close reference to text

A ANALYSIS

These are useful, especially in the early stages of practising essay writing or if you are nervous on the day of your exam. However, be careful about relying too heavily on a formulaic approach. For example, one paragraph might need two or three quotations whereas another paragraph, none. The important thing is that you answer the question by showing knowledge and understanding, analysis skills and evaluation skills. At Higher level, you should be aiming to produce a confident, flowing piece that demonstrates your critical writing skills.

How is the critical essay marked?

Look at the table on the next page, which SQA examiners will use to mark your critical essay.

Marks	20–19	18–16	15–13	12–10	9–6	5–1	0
Knowledge and understanding The critical essay demonstrates:	• a comprehensive knowledge and understanding of the text • a comprehensive selection of textual evidence to support a relevant and coherent argument	• a very clear knowledge and understanding of the text • very clear textual evidence to support an argument which is clearly focused on the demands of the question	• a clear knowledge and understanding of the text • clear textual understanding to support the demands of the question	• an adequate knowledge and understanding of the text • adequate textual evidence to support a line of thought which has some focus on the question	• limited evidence of knowledge and understanding of the text • limited textual evidence to support focus on the demands of the question	• little knowledge and understanding of the text • little textual evidence to support focus on the demands of the question	
Analysis The critical essay demonstrates:	• a comprehensive analysis of the effect of features of language/filmic techniques	• a very clear analysis of the effect of features of language/filmic techniques	• a clear analysis of the effect of features of language/filmic techniques	• an adequate analysis of the effect of features of language/filmic techniques	• limited analysis of the effect of features of language/filmic techniques	• little analysis of features of language/filmic techniques	
Evaluation The critical essay demonstrates:	• a committed, very clear evaluative stance with respect to the text and the task	• a very clear evaluative stance with respect to the text and the task	• a clear evaluative stance with respect to the text and the task	• adequate evidence of an evaluative stance with respect to the text and the task	• limited evidence of an evaluative stance with respect to the text and the task	• little evidence of an evaluative stance with respect to the text and the task	

A closer look at questions

Task

On your own or with a partner

1. Choose a genre you are studying for the Critical Essay part of your exam.
2. Read through the three questions in your chosen genre. These have been taken or adapted from the SQA specimen paper (a paper put together to help teachers and pupils prepare for the exam). Think about the text(s) you have studied for your Higher exam.
3. Put each question into one of three categories in relation to the texts you have studied:
   A. definitely good
   B. reasonable
   C. tricky for your text.

The SQA's aim is that you will find something you can tackle readily on whichever text you have studied.

Drama

First, look at the general instruction. This is displayed in a box at the top of the Drama section. It reminds you to refer to the text and lists the key features to include in your analysis of the play.

> *Answers to questions on Drama should refer to the text and to such relevant features as characterisation, key scene(s), structure, climax, theme, plot, conflict, setting ...*

Points to note:

- The list is fairly obvious – the key features of a drama you will know well by the time of your exam. There is nothing there to catch you out.

- It says 'such relevant features as' and ends with an ellipsis. This means that you do not have to cover them all *and* that you might wish to consider other features too. It is an instruction designed to support you, not restrict what you want to say.

Examples of questions

1. Choose a play in which a central character struggles to cope with social convention, financial difficulties or family duties. Briefly explain the reasons for the character's struggle and discuss how the dramatist's presentation of this struggle enhances your understanding of character and/or theme in the play as a whole.
2. Choose a play in which the concluding scene provides effective clarification of the central concerns. By referring in detail to the concluding scene, discuss in what ways it is important for your understanding of the play as a whole.
3. Choose a play in which the conflict between two characters is an important feature. Briefly explain the nature of this conflict and discuss how the dramatist's presentation of this feature enhances your understanding of the play as a whole.

Task

With a partner or in small groups

Choose one of the above questions and try planning an essay to answer it, using your knowledge of a play you have studied.

Example of a critical essay

As this book has focused on *Men Should Weep*, we will consider how well the three questions above fit this play. Remember that you would only be writing an essay on *Men Should Weep*, if you have studied another text from the SQA list for your Scottish Text section. Any of the questions above would work for *Men Should Weep*, but the one that leaps out, perhaps, is question 1. Read it again, paying particular attention to the highlighted words.

> Choose a play in which a central character struggles to cope with social convention, financial difficulties or family duties. Briefly explain the reasons for the character's struggle and discuss how the dramatist's presentation of this struggle enhances your understanding of character and/or theme in the play as a whole.

This is an ideal question for *Men Should Weep*: the central character, Maggie, faces financial difficulties that dominate her life, and the theme of poverty is a major feature of the text. In fact, you cannot possibly say all there is to say in 45 minutes (the time you have for your critical essay). The question offers you three possibilities: to focus on character or theme, or both.

The following essay plan focuses on character. This is one way to answer the question: of course, there are others. Paragraphs 1 (Introduction) and 2 ('Briefly explain the reasons for the character's struggle') have been written in full, but the rest of the essay is in plan format.

> Note that the paragraphs in the following examples have been given letters simply to identify them. In your critical essay you should not give any of the paragraphs letters or numbers.

1. In *Men Should Weep* by Ena Lamont Stewart, Maggie Morrison, the central character, struggles with financial difficulties. Set in Glasgow in the 1930s, the play focuses on Maggie's attempts to create a good life for her family, despite the relentless, crushing poverty they live in. This struggle dominates the action of the play and helps to define the character of Maggie. She is a matriarchal figure who supports and cares for three generations of her family in a small tenement flat and who, though often battling against overwhelming challenges and sometimes discouraged, demonstrates the heroism of which the human spirit is capable.

2. The play is set during the 1930s Depression, when millions throughout the world were out of work and living in poverty. The East End of Glasgow was a particularly troubled area, with poverty, crime and social deprivation prevalent. Maggie's husband, John, is unemployed and, although Maggie has a cleaning job, there is very little money. Their situation is worsened by the size of their family: children ranging from young adult to Christopher the baby. Granny (John's mother) also lives with them part of the time, and the oldest son, Alec (also unemployed), and his wife, Isa, move in temporarily, after their own home collapses.

The rest of the question asks you to discuss how the dramatist's presentation of this struggle enhances your understanding of character and/or theme in the play as a whole. This is the most important part of the essay. The bullet points in the plan below suggest one way of approaching it.

➡

3. Maggie's defining characteristic of heroism is determined by poverty:

- Perseverance, despite physical and emotional exhaustion (plus examples).
- Self-denial (plus examples).

4. Maggie has taken on the traditional female role of carer for the various characters with whom she comes into contact:

- Granny.
- The children.
- Providing a home for Alec and Isa.

5. Tensions rise in the family under financial strain and Maggie attempts to keep the peace while remaining loyal to John and their relationship:

- The role of Lily.
- Conflict between John and Jenny.
- Let down by John's siding with Isa.

6. Inevitably, the multiple pressures resulting from their poverty become too much for Maggie at times: we see her lose control (she is a heroic character but very human):

- Key moment in Act 2 (end) – why does it happen? What do we learn about her?
- Climax: humiliation of John – why does it happen? What do we learn about him?

7. Maggie's strength at the end of the play is demonstrated when she asserts herself and takes charge of her and her family's lives. The catalyst is, again, money:

- Explain Jenny's offer.
- Bertie's situation: he cannot come home to a squalid house.
- Determination to stand up to John and put the family first.
- Optimism at the end.

8. Conclusion: return to the wording of the question: Maggie's character is dominated by the struggle with financial hardship. Sum up your main points.

Prose: fiction

First, look at the general instruction. This is displayed in a box at the top of the Prose section. It reminds you to refer to the text and lists the key features to include in your analysis of the text.

> *Answers to questions on prose fiction should refer to the text and to such relevant features as characterisation, setting, language, key incident(s), climax, turning point, plot, structure, narrative technique, theme, ideas, description ...*

Points to note:

- As with drama, there is nothing surprising in this list. They are all typical prose features you are likely to know.
- Again, 'such relevant features as' means that your essay does not have to include every feature and you may deal with others not mentioned in the box.

Examples of questions

1. Choose a novel or short story in which there is a disturbing or violent incident. Explain briefly what happens during this incident and discuss to what extent the disturbing or violent nature of the incident is important to your understanding of the text as a whole.

2. Choose a novel or short story in which a particular setting is crucial. Briefly describe the setting and discuss how this feature is used to enhance your appreciation of the text as a whole.

3. Choose a novel or short story in which a central character is presented as a menacing or threatening presence. Discuss how the writer's presentation of this character adds to your understanding of the text as a whole.

Task

With a partner or in small groups

Choose one of the above questions and try planning an essay to answer it, using your knowledge of a prose text you have studied.

Example of a critical essay

As this book has focused on *Sunset Song* and the short stories of George Mackay Brown, we will consider how to plan an essay on these. Remember that you would only be writing an essay on either of these if you have studied another text from the SQA list for your Scottish Text section. Any of the above questions would work for both *Sunset Song* and George Mackay Brown's short stories. We are going to try:

*   question 1: *Sunset Song*

*   question 2: George Mackay Brown

although you could easily attempt these the other way round.

Read question 1 again, paying particular attention to the highlighted words.

> Choose a novel or short story in which there is a disturbing or violent incident. Explain briefly what happens during this incident and discuss to what extent the disturbing or violent nature of the incident is important to your understanding of the text as a whole.

Here is a sample essay for *Sunset Song*, which has been written in full.

Be clear about the question and, in this case, link it to the incident in question and its later theme.

A disturbing incident in the novel *Sunset Song* by Lewis Grassic Gibbon occurs when Ewan Tavendale, husband of the heroine Chris, returns home on embarkation leave following military training during the First World War. Set in the Mearns of Scotland, the novel charts the development of Chris from teenage girl to mature woman, with her marriage to and loss of Ewan dominating the climactic section 'Harvest'. Ewan's transformation from loving husband to drunken, violent brute is significant in terms of character and narrative development, precipitating the climax of the novel. Crucially, it also illustrates the novel's key theme: change.

→

A brief summary of the incident is useful – it can then be referred to.

Guilty and confused about enlisting and deserting his family, Ewan has left for training with neither explanation nor goodbye. Chris puts the upset of this behind her, and anticipates his embarkation leave with excitement and love, only to be bitterly disappointed. Encountering this coarsened and brutalised new version of Ewan, Chris is at first traumatised and lost before she regains her cool inner control. This is not the man she loved – and she closes the door of her heart on him. This time when he leaves it is she who does not say goodbye.

This now links to the incident's effect on character.

Ewan's 'change' is Grassic Gibbon's way of describing the devastating effects of war at a personal level. Training in itself, preparation for conflict, has been enough to divorce Ewan from his deeper emotions. Now he turns the previous sharing and gentleness of their love-making into something 'foul', as Chris thinks of it, and his tenderness towards young Ewan is replaced by cruel impatience and neglect. She tries to rationalise this: 'it wasn't Ewan, her Ewan, someone coarse and strange had come back in his body to torment her'.

Developing into further effect on character, plot and theme.

In turn, this leads to the emergence of a Chris whom we have previously seen foreshadowed – for example, after the death of her father – a Chris who can find the inner strength to turn her back on those who have mistreated her, whose steely, even cold, determination will safeguard herself, her son, her farm. Ewan's blustering threats are met with a kitchen knife and his apparent conviction that Chris's love will survive his contempt is proved wrong: no last-minute reconciliation takes place. Once he has gone, again, as with her father, Chris remembers the old Ewan and is ravaged by guilt at what she has done. From then on, however, she simply buries herself in the practical running of the farm and the raising of young Ewan, sparing no time to think. Her absorption in the land now is not what it once was, for determination and need have replaced joy. In the fullness of time she herself will accept this change and leave the land. However, for now, she has 'turned to the land, close to it and the smell of it … it was not cruel'.

Links between plot, character and their relationship.

Ewan's destructively uncharacteristic behaviour will affect the plot even more profoundly, however. His memory of it comes to haunt him when he is in France, in the battle zone. The guilt-induced misery that expressed itself in his hardening of emotions now leads to his desertion. The doomed, futile gesture of setting off home to Chris – and therefore sacrificing his life – shows us how deeply his betrayal of the family he loves has affected him. When Chris learns of his desertion and execution from Chae Strachan, a soldier neighbour, she is able to forgive Ewan, to be proud of his sacrifice 'for me and Blawearie, my dear, my dear', and to reconcile emotionally with his spirit.

→

Finally, and importantly, the influence of this incident on the novel's theme.

This makes a gripping and moving link with the novel's central theme of change, with the idea that 'nothing endures'. The traditional way of life of the small crofter seemed to have an improved, viable future in the hands of educated, dedicated folk like Chris, but this attractive vision of a regenerated lifestyle has proved false. War has swept it away.

In this way, Ewan himself has been a symbol – a traditional farmer, bonded to the soil – but in his youthfulness and marriage to Chris, representative of the future. His death, along with that of a generation of the area's more enlightened, idealistic crofters, marks the end of a way of life that had one foot in the past and one in the future. What will follow will be something very different – for the Mearns and for Scotland – and Grassic Gibbon warns that this future must not be a soulless commercialism, lacking the small-scale humanity of the past.

In the Conclusion, return to the question and sum up what you have discussed so far.

We can see therefore that this disturbing incident, in its disruptive effect, is a clear turning point for character and plot, pointing the way to ultimate tragedy. In the way in which it echoes huge events happening at international level, it prepares us for the great sense of loss that pervades *Sunset Song*'s conclusion and helps us to understand its theme of change.

Read question 2 again, paying particular attention to the highlighted words.

Choose a novel or short story in which a particular setting is crucial. Briefly describe the setting and discuss how this feature is used to enhance your appreciation of the text as a whole.

The critical essay, based on George Mackay Brown's 'A Time to Keep', has been planned as follows. You could begin it like this:

1. Introduction: In the short story 'A Time to Keep' by George Mackay Brown, the setting of the small island community, over the course of one year, is crucial.

   - The setting is not just a background but integral to development of plot, character and theme.

   - Importance of nature: weather, the changing seasons, the sea in influencing the lives of main characters.

   - Setting also involves the community, the collective opinion of the people the main characters live with.

   - Setting helps develop characters, plot and theme of humanity's struggle in a harsh and uncaring world.

➡

2. Briefly describe the setting:

- Isolated community: importance of nature; human life dependent on weather/seasons/sea.
- Physically demanding way of life, coping with the elements and farming under difficult conditions.
- Randomly destructive natural events, e.g. storm destroying lobster pots, rain destroying harvest – key moments in story.
- Community support vital in these difficult circumstances: help each other out at key moments in the year (e.g. harvest) and life (e.g. childbirth, death) but Bill and Ingi are isolated from this, mainly because of Bill's refusal to conform.

Now for the main part of the essay:

Discuss how this feature is used to enhance your appreciation of the text as a whole.

You might plan this part as follows:

3. Impact of setting on plot:

- Opening places: main characters in middle of a wintry scene, walking ten miles from wedding reception to their new home.
- Details of opening which make clear the crucial role the setting plays.
- Narrative develops over (almost) a year in life of Bill and Ingi: builds to a climax of the 'harvest' of their child's birth/but death of Ingi.

4. Impact of setting on character development: focus on Bill:

- Harsh life/failure as crofter, e.g. death of lambs.
- Starts off full of hope/other external (and internal) factors causing him to change.

5. Bill and the community – his refusal to conform isolates him and Ingi:

- Religion – Bill rejects this.
- Not helping with harvest due to earlier confrontation over lobster pots.
- Not spending time with other men.

6. Impact of community on relationship of Bill and Ingi:

- Passionate, mutually exclusive – no need for others, yet community provides support and they lack this.
- She is lonely and isolated/only friend Anna.
- Role of her father – small community, he is comparatively wealthy; seeks to control.

7. Role of community at climax of story – death of Ingi:

- Bill's refusal to be hypocritical and accept comfort of religious platitudes.
- Bill reaches an uneasy acceptance of community at end.

8. Conclusion

Task

On your own

If you are studying the work of George Mackay Brown, try writing the critical essay for question 2 using this plan. If you are studying another writer, use the plan as a template for your answer.

Poetry

First, look at the general instruction. This is displayed in a box at the top of the Poetry section. It reminds you to refer to the text and lists the key features to include in your analysis of the poem.

> *Answers to questions on Poetry should refer to the text and to such relevant features as word choice, tone, imagery, structure, content, rhythm, rhyme, theme, sound, ideas ...*

Points to note:

- As with drama and prose, there is nothing surprising in this list. They are all typical features of poetry that you should have encountered before.

- Again, 'such relevant features as' means that your essay does not have to include every feature and you may deal with others not mentioned in the box, such as the verse forms used by Burns.

Examples of questions

1. Choose a poem in which the poet expresses his or her feelings about a person, place or issue. Discuss how the poet's use of language contributes to the overall effect of the poem.
2. Choose two poems that deal with the same theme. Discuss how the theme is explored in each poem and explain which poem you believe offers a more memorable exploration of the theme.
3. Choose a poem that features a relationship. Discuss how the poet's presentation of this relationship adds to your understanding of the central concern(s) of the poem.

Task

With a partner or in small groups

Choose one of the above questions and try planning an essay to answer it, using your knowledge of the poetry you have studied.

Example of a critical essay

As this book has focused on Robert Burns and Liz Lochhead, we will consider how the above questions would work for these poets. Remember that you would only be writing an essay on either of these if you have studied another text from the SQA list for your Scottish Text section. We are going to try:

- question 1: Robert Burns
- question 3: Liz Lochhead

although you could easily do these the other way round.

Read question 1 again, paying attention to the highlighted words.

> Choose a poem in which the poet expresses his or her feelings about a person, place or issue. Discuss how the poet's use of language contributes to the overall effect of the poem.

This is an ideal question for 'A Man's a Man for A' That'. Read the approach outlined below and the sample essay that follows.

- Feelings about an issue: Burns's belief that genuine human qualities are much more important than rank or privilege.

- Approach: using the notes on 'A Man's a Man for A' That' in this book, plan the stages of your essay as follows:
  - Introduction: refer to topic and poem.
  - Explain Burns's use of contrast to show his speaker's disdain for rank, along with his love of 'sense' and 'worth'.
  - Deal with his attack on respect for privilege.
  - Show how he builds up the positive.
  - Conclusion/climax of poem.
  - Conclusion of essay.

Here is a sample essay for 'A Man's a Man for A' That', which has been written in full.

Introduce your topic and justify your choice of text.	'A Man's a Man for A' That' is a resounding, authentic piece of poetry in which Robert Burns lets his feelings be fully known. Though highly political in terms of its reference to class differences, it is his burning love for decent, ordinary human values and qualities which provides the poem's passion, conveyed effectively through a range of poetic techniques.
Provide a clear stance and a sense of overall 'argument' of essay.	One of the poem's achievements is its perfect balance between contrasting elements as the speaker denounces the worship of the rich and powerful while simultaneously building towards the poem's final crescendo: its 'hymn' of praise for 'sense and worth' and brotherhood.
In poetry essays, bring in textual detail quickly. Analysis is an important aspect of an essay on this genre.	The negative aspect is expressed to some extent through briefly sketched but striking visual images. The first is that of 'the coward slave' who 'hangs his head'. The speaker makes it very clear that there should be no shame in 'honest poverty': no head-hanging in the presence of self-indulgent 'fools ... and knaves' and their 'tinsel show'. Burns's word choice shows that there is to be no compromise. 'Tinsel show' may catch the eye and impress, but there is nothing real about it. The 'guinea's stamp' is valueless in itself – only a superficial moulding, which is how we should view rank or wealth. The 'gowd', the human being, is all that matters.
	This prepares for the bold, provocative image that dominates the heart of the poem:
Quotation which can then be referred to later.	'Ye see yon birkie ca'd a lord,
	Wha struts an' stares, an' a' that;
	Tho' hundreds worship at his word,
	He's but a coof for a' that:'

Or build quotations into the text.	The dismissive contempt in the choice of 'birkie' and 'coof' to describe Burns's generic example of a man of power is given an edge by 'ca'd a lord'. Like the 'guinea's stamp' and 'tinsel show', it has nothing to do with inner quality and is simply a label. The 'birkie' 'struts an' stares, an' a' that'. There is a sense here of him going nowhere and actually looking at nothing: these are merely posturing attitudes. Alliteration emphasises the key words 'struts' and 'stares' while 'an a' that', in this context, seems to imply all the other nonsense that occupies his time. All these language features emphasise his ridiculousness.
Comment on the impact of your quotation.	
Make fluent and clear links between paragraphs, which show how a line of thought is being developed.	The riposte to this comes in the stanza's final lines: 'The man o' independent mind / He looks an' laughs at a' that.' This 'independent mind' ('independent' is, noticeably, the poem's longest word) is the counter to the mindless adoration given to the 'birkie' as 'hundreds worship at his word'. In one direct comparison, this man does not 'stare' but 'looks' and, we take it, actually sees and understands. The alliteration in 'looks an' laughs at a' that' creates its own powerful visual snapshot, showing us how best to respond to the nonsense of the lord's pride.
Keep referring to techniques: avoid becoming too 'narrative'.	It is this sense of unintimidated, unimpressed self-esteem that Burns seeks to create at the end of each stanza. 'The Man' stands for all of us ordinary folk, male or female. We are the 'gowd' in the guinea: each one of us (if honest) is 'king o' men' – and of 'higher rank' – than those whom the king can entitle. Thus, after the satirical invective of each stanza is done, a bright, optimistic, positive declaration bursts through.
Helpful to refer to structure in a poetry essay.	This is, in effect, the structure of the poem itself, as the final stanza casts aside denunciation, to invite its listeners in: 'Then let us pray that come it may, / (As come it will for a' that.)'. 'We' are made an integral part of things as the poem's first inner rhyme ('pray'/'may') swings us into the anthem of the final stanza. The word choice of the simple, unadorned 'Sense and Worth' and the use of Scots idiom, 'Shall bear the gree', reminds us of the poem's roots even as its message reaches out from Scotland 'o'er a' the earth' and 'the world o'er'. There is a certain caution in the word 'may', but it is the driving certainty of 'As come it will' and 'It's coming yet' that blazes through in the climactic prophecy that all people 'Shall brothers be for a' that'.
Return to the question: summarise the main points made in your essay.	In conclusion, this is a powerful, heartfelt piece of work in which Burns expresses his feelings about what really matters in a person. Burns's great skill has gone into producing one of the most effective clarion calls of hope and of faith in the human spirit. Absolute simplicity of language and a virtuosic balance of elements have allowed this poem's strength of feeling to communicate its message across the centuries and over national and cultural boundaries.

Read question 3 again, paying attention to the highlighted words.

Choose a poem that features a relationship. Discuss how the poet's presentation of this relationship adds to your understanding of the central concern(s) of the poem.

What is this question actually asking you to do? Once you have chosen an appropriate poem – Liz Lochhead's 'My Rival's House' would work very well – you are asked to focus on two things:

- how the relationship is presented: a close examination of poetic techniques

- link these to central concerns: themes.

In fact, these are not separate tasks: they will intertwine throughout the essay. The following plan is one possible way to answer this question. It is based on 'My Rival's House' by Liz Lochhead.

1. Introduction: in 'My Rival's House', Liz Lochhead tackles a relationship which teeters on the brink of all-out conflict from the start, and yet which must try to sustain itself. A new girlfriend, the poem's persona, visits her partner's possessive, controlling mother and becomes very aware of the difficulties she will face.

2. House as symbol for mother's attitude:
   - Look at perfection/lack of true welcome.

3. Examples of techniques which emphasise unfriendly, over-perfect 'surfaces':
   - List, word choice, sound, enjambment, rhyme.

4. Girlfriend's sense of inferiority/intimidation:
   - Superficial manners, smooth rhythm.

5. Portrayal of what 'squirms' beneath mother's surface:
   - Rhythm breaking up, use of enhanced cliché, repetition.

6. How mother's feelings start coming to surface:
   - Insect/meal metaphors.

7. Conclusion:
   - Skill in creating of mother/response of speaker – showing how some relationships can never succeed.

> Paragraph 4 gives an example of how to use textual detail. The speaker begins to think of herself, ironically, as superficial and lacking substance:
>
> 'I am all edges, a surface, a shell
> and yet my rival thinks she means me well.'
>
> In the first line, reflecting her nervousness, the rhythm is broken by the use of short phrases. The first metaphor, 'all edges', suggests her acute discomfort; the second, using the poem's central word 'surface', seems to reduce her to the level of furniture, while 'shell' suggests both emptiness and brittleness. The second line, referring to the mother's frosty good-manners, returns to a smooth rhythmic flow, emphasising that the mother is very much in control.

Task

On your own

If you are studying the work of Liz Lochhead, try writing the critical essay for question 3 using this plan. If you are studying another poet, use the plan as a template for your answer.